Charles Marvin

**The Russians at the Gates of Herat**

Charles Marvin

**The Russians at the Gates of Herat**

ISBN/EAN: 9783337297121

Printed in Europe, USA, Canada, Australia, Japan

Cover: Foto ©ninafisch / pixelio.de

More available books at **www.hansebooks.com**

THE

# RUSSIANS

AT THE

# GATES OF HERAT.

By CHARLES MARVIN.

*WITH·MAPS AND PORTRAITS.*

NEW YORK:
GEORGE MUNRO, PUBLISHER,
17 TO 27 VANDEWATER STREET.

# LIST OF MAPS AND PORTRAITS.

# PREFACE.

In my "Russian Advance Towards India," published in 1882, I made these remarks: " In my writings on Russia I try to be impartial. I know I have a greater love for Russia, the country of my youth, and a better appreciation of the Russian people, than the so-called Russophile ' traders in politics, who lauded her indiscriminately in 1877, from motives of self or party interest, and abandoned her afterward to false attacks: and the public know, from my writ-. ings, that I am a vigilant and anxious observer of the Russian advance toward India. I am thus, I suppose, both a Russophile and a Russophobe. As for my local opinions, my youth was passed in a country which has no political parties corresponding with our Liberal and Conservative factions, and does not want them; while my studies have led me to survey politics from the standpoint of one who considers himself more in the light of a citizen of the English Empire—of that great empire that embraces the five empires of England, of Canada, of Australia, of South Africa, and of India—than merely a Liberal or Conservative Englishman of Lesser England only. Being, in this sense, an Imperialist, and a non-party writer, I claim immunity from any charge of unduly favoring Liberal or Conservative policy in my remarks on the Central Asian Question. At the same time, I would have it with equal clearness understood, that the opinions expressed are not merely the heedless and ephemeral views of an irresponsible writer, but the deep conviction of one who is conscious that they may some day be called up against him, in other spheres than that of Journalism and Literature."

These remarks cover all that I need say by way of a preface to the present volume, except that the entire work having been written and got out in eight days, I may ask indulgence for any errors that may have escaped my eye in the volume.

CHARLES MARVIN.

GROSVENOR HOUSE,
    PLUMSTEAD COMMON, KENT,
      *March 23d*, 1885.

# THE RUSSIANS AT THE GATES OF HERAT.

## CHAPTER 1.

### HOW ALIKHANOFF FIRST WENT TO MERV.

The landing of the Russians at Krasnovodsk—Early Turcoman campaigns—
Alikhanoff joins Lomakin's army as a private soldier—Acts as special correspondent of the *Moscow Gazette*—Skobeleff's siege of Geok Tepé—Russia
determines to secure a military survey of Merv—Alikhanoff proceeds to
the oasis disguised as a trader—How he obtained plans of the fortress—Per-
suades Makdum Kuli, the principal Merv warrior, to attend the Czar's coronation at Moscow.

THERE are two Russian movements in the direction of India.
One originated at Orenburg, and had for its objective Cabul.
Commencing before the Crimean war it rapidly developed itself
afterward, and ingulfed in succession the Kirghez tribes and the
khanates of Khokand, Bokhara, and Khiva. Practically speaking,
this movement ceased shortly before the last Turkish war, and has
not been continued since. The interest in Turkestan for the moment, therefore, being purely historical, we may exclude an account
of the advance in the direction of Cabul from this volume.

The second movement was from the Caspian, and had for its objective Herat. A deal of confusion and bad statesmanship has arisen
from confounding this advance with that made from Orenburg and
Tashkent. The troops, have been always different, the officials
different, and conditions regulating the advance different. We have
only to specify one popular error to show how essential it is that
the public should clearly realize the difference between the two
movements. For instance, it is often said that colossal mountain
ranges bar the Russian advance to the Indian frontier. This is
quite true as regards troops marching from Tashkent and Samar-
cara upon Cabul and Peshawur. The lofty Hindoo Koosh, that
must be traversed to reach the Ameer's capital, ranges in height
from 15,000 to 20,000 feet. But there is nothing of the kind between
the Caspian and Herat, nor yet again between Herat and the Indo-
Afghan frontier. Setting out from Krasnovodsk, a Russian could
drive a four-in-hand all the way to the Indian frontier near Quetta.

If this fact be clearly borne in mind, the reader will readily
understand how rapid the Russian advance has been since Skobeleff broke down the Turcoman barrier, and how essential it is that
the disadvantage of there being no physical obstacle to a powerful
military movement from the Caspian should not be enhanced by
allowing Russia to secure the great midway camping ground of
Herat.

In the time of Peter the Great, and again in the reign of Nicholas, Russia seized points on the East Caspian Coast, but the so-called Caspian advance toward India did not definitely commence until a descent was made upon Krasnovodsk in 1869. In the autumn of that year a flotilla left the Caucasus port of Petrovsk, and landed on the opposite side of the Caspian a few Cossacks and infantrymen, and half a dozen guns. Attached to this expedition were three men who subsequently figured prominently in Central Asian history. One was Stolictoff, the envoy Russia sent to Cabul in 1878; the second Grodekoff, who made a famous ride to Herat in the same year, and the third Captain Skobeleff, then a harum-scarum subaltern.

"We made a great mistake when we landed at Krasnovodsk," said the latter to me, shortly before his death. "Instead of going ahead we dawdled about, reconnoitering the country. A strong forward movement was not approved of by the Government. The result was, we gradually taught the Turcomans how to fight, and at last they fought so well that it needed a series of great campaigns to crush them."

Our space is too limited to describe in detail those reconnoiterings and skirmishes which, during the period from 1869 to 1878, converted the Tekke Turcoman from an undisciplined horseman into a skillful builder of big redoubts. No headway whatever was made after. Skobeleff left in 1873 to join the expedition to Khiva, and a long series of reverses culminated in a crushing defeat and rout of the Russians at Geok Tepé in the autumn of 1879.

This was the campaign in which two notable personages participated—Mr. Edmund O'Donovan, and Private Alikhanoff. The former was attached to General Lazareff's force, and spent the whole of the summer in the Caspian. Unluckily he fell ill when the advance took place, and was thus debarred from seeing anything of the fighting. What we know of the campaign is mainly derived from the letters of a few Russians attached to the force. The best appeared in the columns of the *Moscow Gazette*, and were signed "Arsky." The writer was Alikhanoff, the present Governor of Merv.*

This Alikhanoff is a very remarkable man. He was born at Baku, and by birth is a Daghestani. Russia's Asiatic subjects have a happy way of identifying themselves with their masters, which our language renders impossible in the case of India—they turn their names into Russian ones, by placing an "off" (son) at the end of them. Alikhanoff is simply Ali Khan, with an "off" added to it. When Sir Peter Lumsden proceeded to the Afghan frontier, he took with him from London a very accomplished Indian official as interpreter, also, curiously enough, one "Ali Khan." But England had failed to effect such a transformation in her Ali Khan as Russia has with hers. I saw him depart from Charing Cross. He was highly educated and thoroughly devoted to England; but he had never thought of identifying himself with us by changing his name from Ali Khan into Mr. Alikhanson, or, better still, Mr. Alison.

The case is totally different in Russia's Asiatic provinces. The peo-

* See "The Disastrous Russian Campaign against the Turcomans." London: W. H. Allen & Co., 1880.

ple not only identify themselves with the Russians, but the Russians identify themselves with the people Englishmen would never think of, placing their home army under a Sikh or a Mahratta, or permitting a Bengali to become a Cabinet Minister. An Indian has practically no career in England. On the other hand, every avenue in Russia is open to the Caucasian. The Armenian, Louis Melikoff, rises there to a position next to that of the Czar. Generals Tergoukasoff and Lazareff, two other Asiatics, commanded Russian troops in the Turkish war of 1877-78, and when Alikhanoff accomplished his famous raid upon Merv, the exploit is extolled as a Russian exploit, and not as the achievement of a mere native.

Alikhanoff received a good education, and developed a remarkable talent for drawing. Skillful with pen and pencil, had he lived in England he would have doubtless become one of the foremost correspondents of the day. At an early age he entered the army, and after serving in the Khivan expedition as a captain of the cavalry under Skobeleff, received the appointment of aide-de-camp to the Grand Duke Michael, Viceroy of the Caucasus. At the close of the Turkish war he suddenly fell into disgrace. A quarrel occurred between him and a superior officer, and he challenged him to fight a duel. The true particulars of this affair have never publicly transpired. Some say Alikhanoff was a boisterous officer, given to insulting people when in his cups, others that his superior officer was a scamp, hated by everybody in the regiment. Whichever story was current, Alikhanoff was tried by court-martial, deprived of all his appointments, and decorations, and reduced to the condition of a common soldier.

"You need to measure soldiers by a different standard from that which you apply to civilians," said Skobeleff to the writer in 1882. "I have had much experience in warfare, and have found that the men who fight best are precisely those who are apt to be troublesome in time of peace. A government should be always very indulgent to its troops in time of peace. Those who are most difficult to deal with in time of peace often prove to be the best fighters in time of war."

Skobeleff's remarks referred to General Valentine Baker, whom he characterized as our "one good general." We were discussing the different modes of treating officers in disgrace adopted by England and Russia. In England we dismiss an officer who has made a false step from the army, and, however good a man he may be professionally, he is practically lost to the country. In Russia, on the other hand, he is simply reduced to the ranks, stripped of his titles, and sent to some frontier district in Asia to serve as a private soldier. Such a man naturally becomes a desperado, and forms capital material for leaders of the stamp of Alikhanoff. In many cases they retrieve their reputation, and it is the custom, if they display extraordinary courage, or render any particular service, to restore them at a stroke to their former position. This was done in the case of Alikhanoff, when he successfully accomplished his swoop upon Merv. It is obvious that the presence of such inflammable materials on the Russian frontier is even far more dangerous to peace than the predatory characteristics of the Afghan tribes Russian diplomats make so much fuss about.

Alikhanoff fell into disgrace about the time General Lomakin returned to the Caspian from an unsuccessful attack upon the Tekke strongholds in Akhal. He at once elected to be sent to Tchikishlar to join the expedition General Lazareff was preparing to lead against the tribesmen. There he met O'Donovan, and one of the last letters that lamented correspondent wrote to me before proceeding to the Soudan contained a request that I should give his hearty wishes to Alikhanoff if I met him during my journey in the Caspian. He said Alikhanoff was a "capital fellow, a brave and capable soldier, and much liked in the camp."

During this campaign Alikhanoff attained the highest rank as a non-commissioned officer. When Skobeleff arrived the following year to retrieve the broken fortunes of the Lazareff-Lomakin expedition, he was accorded every opportunity of distinguishing himself. However, attached to the force were so many heroes, as dashing as himself, that his exploits were lost among the crowd of great achievements.

The history of Skobeleff's siege of Geok Tepé yet remains to be written. O'Donovan saw nothing of it, except the final rout, through a telescope from a hill on the Perso-Turcoman frontier. Hence he left it undescribed in his book on Merv. None the less, it was a campaign full of exciting incident, and a clear account of it would be very popular in this country.

Retreating from their line of settlements, stretching along the Akhal frontier, from Kizil Arvat to Geok Tepé, the Tekkes collected to the number of 40,000 families at the latter place, and forming a camp, with tents pitched closely one against the other, built round it a huge clay wall, reminding the Russians of an immense railway embankment. The defense was mainly controlled by two chiefs, Mahdum Kuli Khan and Tekme Sardar. The latter had submitted to Russia the year before, but being badly treated by Lomakin, had fled the camp and joined his countrymen afresh. There he instructed in the art of building rapidly large earthworks, after the manner he had observed practiced by the Russians during their advance.

The expedition the previous year had been dispatched up the Atrek River, from its mouth at Tchikishlar. Skobeleff changed the base to Krasnovodsk, or more properly to Port-Mechaelovsk, a small harbor on the south-east side of Krasnovodsk; and considerably nearer Akhal. It is from this point that the railway now runs in the direction of India.

At that time the Turcoman barrier was considered so difficult to break down that Russia was ready to resort to extraordinary efforts to hasten the submission of the tribes. During the debates on Candahar, Lord Salisbury said that he had always believed that the Turcoman barrier would last his life-time. Even in Russia, so severe was the resistance apprehended, that General Tergoukasoff, Skobeleff's predecessor, did not think that the barrier could be broken with less than three years' hard fighting. To quicken matters, Russia therefore selected Skobeleff for the task, and very wisely gave him *carte blanche* as to the resources he was to employ to accomplish it.

Stowed away in the magazines at Bender, on the south-west fron-

tier, were one hundred miles of railway, which Russia had purchased to use in the Balkan campaign in the event of a failure of
the Berlin Congress. At Skobeleff's request, the material was
shifted to the Caspian, and laid down in the direction of Geok
Tepé. In this casual manner originated the Russian railway to India, which has effected so many changes in Central Asia, and prom-

GENERAL KOUROPATKIN.

ises to completely revolutionize the relations of England and Russia
with the region.

The railway, however, proved of very little service in the actual
campaign, and we must, therefore, reserve an account of it for a
future chapter. While it was being built Skobeleff pushed on a
force to Bami, the first stronghold of any size in the Akhal oasis,
and there gradually accumulated the munitions of war and food supplies essential for the siege. When everything was ready he ad-

vanced to Geok Tepé, and, seizing a fortified point close to the walls, commenced attack upon the fortress.

The Tekke stronghold was fully as difficult to take as the Russians had expected. Their artillery made no impression with the huge clay rampart; they had to resort to every form of siege operations to reduce the fortress  The conflict lasted nearly a month, during which the Russians suffered heavy losses, and experienced severe privations. Step by step, however, Skobeleff pushed his way until he got close enough to sink a mine, which was carried to the foot of the rampart. At the same time, his 69 guns fired daily from 100 to 500 shots into the place, and the expenditure of ammunition by the infantry ranged from 10,000 to 70,000 rounds a day.

The brunt of the attack fell upon General Kouropatkin, commanding the Turkestan Contingent. As this officer is spoken of as likely to command the Russian arms, in the event of a conflict at the gates of Herat, it may be well to take advantage of the opportunity to say a few words about him.

Among rising Russian generals, there is probably no one more admired by the army than Kouropatkin. He was Skobeleff's right-hand man in most of his campaigns. He served with him in the Khivan expedition, and in the Khokandese campaign. He acted as chief of his staff at Plevna, and during the march upon Constantinople, and he exercised immediate control, under Skobeleff, of the forces before Geok Tepé.

When Skobeleff was appointed to the charge of the army against the Turcomans, one of his first acts was to telegraph to Kouropatkin, then in the Kuldja frontier, to join him with a contingent of Turkestan troops. His march across Central Asia excited universal admiration at the time. After being weeks on the road, proceeding from Tashkent to Khiva, Kouropatkin had to accomplish a difficult march across the desert, by a route almost unknown, to the concentrating point of Bami. General Annenkoff was at Bami at the time and went out to meet him. "Kouropatkin," he said to me, in dilating enthusiastically on this achievement—"Kouropatkin had been twenty-six days marching over a sandy and waterless desert: yet his force marched in clean and trim, and as fresh as a daisy."

When, at the invitation of Skobeleff's friends, I accompanied the funeral party, conveying the body of that great hero from Moscow to its last resting-place at Spasskoe Selo, in South Russia, in 1882, I was thrown for several days among Skobeleff's favorite officers; and more than once I heard a controversy among them as to whether Kouropatkin was not almost as good a leader as their lost general. "Kouropatkin," said a Turkestan officer to me during one of these discussions, "possesses all the characteristics of Skobeleff, cast in a cooler mold. They worked admirably together, Kouropatkin imparting coolness and calculation to Skobeleff, and Skobeleff fire and enthusiasm to Kouropatkin. I am quite desolate now that Skobeleff is gone "—here his eyes filled with tears—" but it is a consolation to all of us that we have still got Kouropatkin. He is now the Skobeleff of Russia."

During the first few days succeeding Skobeleff's death a strong and angry feeling prevailed in Russia against the Government. It was felt that the deceased hero's merits had never been properly appieciated by the State, and 1 encountered various officers at Moscow who were persuaded he had been poisoned. To appease the army the Emperor felt he could not do better than summon Kouropatkin from Central Asia and give him a high appointment at home. Since then he has been treated as a favorite at Court, and if he has secured no notoriety abroad, it is simply because he has always devoted himself to his profession and left politics alone. Skobeleff had in him all the elements of a great statesman as well as of a great general. His political influence was becoming positively embarrassing to the Czar's ministers when he died. Kouropatkin has never sought to form a party in Russia—he is quite content to be a great general, and nothing more.

During the siege of Geok Tepé he had charge of the advanced positions and displayed extraordinary coolness and courage. Unobtrusive almost to a fault, he carefully supervised the mechanical parts of the siege operations, while Skobeleff applied himself to keeping th troops in that rollicking, reckless mood he considered so valuable in the presence of the enemy. Seated at the mouth of the mine, Skobeleff used to time the progress of the sappers underground tunneling in the direction of the fortress. If the officer in charge accomplished the specified portion in less than the time fixed, he was kissed and caressed, and perhaps treated to champagne or vodky; if the reverse was the case, he was roundly abused before all the soldiers.

Throughout the greater part of the siege Alikhanoff, who was now a cornet of the Pereslaff Dragoons, was employed in foraging operations, or reconnoitering that portion of the fortress facing the desert, which was uninvested by the Russians.

At length the day of the assault arrived. More than a ton of gunpowder was laid at the head of the mine, immediately under the rampart, and, on being fired, laid bare a broad entrance into the enemy's defenses. Through this, and another breach made by the artillery, the Russians rushed into the place, and perpetrated all the horrors usual when orders are given to infuriated and semi-barbarous troops to give no quarter to either sex.

Even when the Turcomans, no longer offering resistance, streamed out in a disorderly mob across the desert in the direction of Merv, men, women, and children mingled together, no mercy was shown to them. Artillery followed in their rear, and mowed them down, until darkness put an end to the pursuit. During that short few hours' chase the 1,000 pursuing Russians slaughtered 8,000 of the fugitives. Hundreds of women were saved: 6,500 bodies were also afterward found under the fortress. At Kertch the year before last I met an Armenian Jew, Samuel Gourovitch, who had accompanied as interpreter a secret Russian mission to Cabul in 1882, and was present at the sack of Geok Tepé. He told me that the carnage was fearful.

"One thousand Russians cut down 8,000 Turcomans in a few hours. The whole country was covered with corpses. The morning after the battle they lay in rows, like freshly mown hay, as they had been swept down by the mitrailleurs and artillery. I myself saw babies bayoneted or slashed to pieces. Many women were ravished before being killed."

" But Skobeleff told me that not a woman had been dishonored."

" Lots were," he replied, energetically.  " They were ravished by the soldiers before my eyes.  Skobeleff may not have known it.  I could tell you many horrible things that took place; but " (tapping his lips significantly) " it is better to be silent in this world.  The plunder at Geok Tepé was immense.  The troops were allowed to get drunk, plunder, and kill for three days after the assault."

During the assault, and in the subsequent pursuit, the infantry engaged fired 278,804 rounds, the cavalry 12,510, and the artillery 5,864 rounds; 224 military rockets were also expended.  The total loss of the Turcomans during the siege was estimated by Skobeleff at 20,000.  In other words half the defenders perished.

The two leaders, Tekme Sardar and Makdum Kuli, escaped, and fled to Merv.  Pushing on their rear, Skobeleff occupied Askabad, the capital of the Akhal Tekkes, twenty-seven miles east of Geok Tepé, and dispatched Kouropatkin thence almost half way to the Merv oasis.  It was these reconnoiterings of Kouropatkin that occasioned so much excitement at the time.  The belief was general that Skobeleff would occupy Merv.

It is almost unnecessary to state that he did not; but it is well to disperse any doubts that may exist as to the reason he did not push on any further.  It is generally supposed that a disinclination to displease England, and a desire to keep his promises, caused the Emperor to restrain the ardor of Skobeleff.  This is a mistake.  By the terrific blow he struck the Akhal Tekkes at Geok Tepé, Skobeleff shattered to pieces the Turcoman barrier Lord Salisbury had fondly believed would last his life-time; but he was too mauled to reap the full advantage of it for the moment.  He only had a striking force of 2,000 men after he occupied Askabad, and having used up nearly all his ammunition during the siege, he was not in a condition to push on to an unknown oasis, and expose himself to a repetition of the hard knocks he had received at Geok Tepé.

So he returned home: but before he left Akhal an incident occurred which shows what a deep personal interest he took in the Central Asian Question.  In spite of Russia's avowed intention of keeping the country she had won, and notwithstanding that the Turcoman barrier had been shattered, the English Government decided to evacuate Afghanistan.  The ablest English writers on the Russo-Indian Question were averse to surrendering Candahar, but the Government persisted in its policy, and it received the warmest concurrence of the Marquis of Ripon.

Speaking at Leeds, on January 28, 1885, the ex-Viceroy said: " We withdrew at a time which suited our purpose, and which we believed to be to the advantage of the Afghan people; and as our troops marched away with steady steps from Candahar, no voice was lifted against us, and no dog barked at our heels."

Yet, as a matter of fact, a voice was lifted against us, and poisoned the motives of our departure.  That voice was Skobeleff's.  In an official account of Skobeleff's campaign, General Grodekoff, the chief of his staff at Geok Tepé, has just published, the following passage occurs: " To raise Russia's *prestige* in Central Asia and to depress that of England, General Skobeleff sent native agents into the bazaars of Central Asia to spread throughout the region the report that it was the White Czar who had compelled England to evacuate Afghanistan."

Such a revelation can not be very pleasing to those who held at the time that we were conciliating Russia by evacuating Candahar. As a matter of fact, our retirement encouraged the Russians to advance. They thought we had had enough of Afghanistan and would never enter the country any more. In an official Russian account of the war which I have in my possession, and which is to be found in every military library in Russia, the writer, General Skobeleff, asserts that we retired because we were so repeatedly defeated by the Afghans that the people of India were excited to a mutinous condition by our disasters. If our army had not fallen back in time the whole of India would have risen against us!

It is the publication of such works as Skobeleff's "Anglo-Afghan Conflict" and Skobeleff's plans for invading India that has stimulated so strongly the desire of Russian military men to upset our Eastern India.

Just before the evacuation of Candahar took place, a clever caricature was published in Russia entitled "England and Russia in Central Asia." This represented two feet: one, English shod, stepping off a piece of ground marked "Afghanistan," and another, incased in a big Russian boot, advancing closely upon it, with the evident intention of administering a kick to the retiring party. I had several thousand copies of this caricature struck off, and distributed them to Parliament and Press during the Candahar debate; but I did not imagine at the time—nor yet, I suppose, did anybody —that the Russian artist had so correctly represented in a sketch meant to be humorous what Skobeleff had actually done.

The brilliant and dashing general having administered a parting kick at us, returned home, and Russia proceeded to organize her new possession. In the meanwhile O'Donovan made his famous dash to Merv, and during his five months' stay wrote those wonderful letters which will never perish so long as any record exists of British travel.

But Mr. O'Donovan did more than simply pen letters to the "Daily News." He endeavored to persuade the Turcomans to cease their attacks upon the Russians and avoid giving them any offense. These efforts were to a large extent successful, and from the time he left the oasis until the Russians occupied it the only outrage the Merv Tekkes perpetrated was the attack on the Parfenoff surveying party in 1882. This outrage, however, was due to some bad characters, and was so quickly and promptly disavowed by the tribe that the Russians expressed themselves perfectly satisfied with the reparation made by the Mervis.

After O'Donovan had left the oasis, the Russian authorities decided they would thoroughly establish their influence there. Tekme Sardar, one of the two Tekke chiefs defending Geok Tepé, had already surrendered to them, and had been sent to St. Petersburg to be tamed by a sight of Russia. The second, Makdum Kuli, O'Donovan's friend, they tried to win over through their secret agents, but failed.

One of these secret agents was Fazil Beg, a Russianized Khivan. He used to go backward and forward between Merv and Askabad and encouraged all the Tekkes he could to visit the latter place to traffic at the bazaar the Russians had erected.

The Russians are well aware of the value of a bazaar as a means of exercising influence in the East. Directly they finished their fort at Askabad, they erected a bazaar there, and encouraged Armenians from Baku and Tiflis to establish shops in it. Before long the Tekkes of Merv, attracted by the high prices the Russians gave for their supplies, began to appear at Askabad, first, singly, and somewhat shy, afterward in bands, when they found they were well treated.

In course of time the richer and more influential of the Mervis followed suit. As all arrivals at the bazaar were notified to the Russian authorities at once, they extended a warm hand to every Tekke who possessed any influence whatever at home, and in this manner created a pro-Russian party at Merv.

Herat is about as close to Merv as Merv is to Askabad. It is well to bear in mind that the moment the Russians occupied Merv they established a bazaar there with Armenian traders from Baku, and commenced applying to the tribesmen of the Murghab those tactics so successful at the capital of the Akhal Tekkes. But for the opportune arrival of Sir Peter Lumsden last autumn there might have already been a pro-Russian party at Herat.

As soon as events had sufficiently matured, the authorities at Askabad decided to send an officer to Merv to obtain secretly a military survey of the oasis. Alikhanoff was the person chosen. To facilitate his operations a caravan was fitted out, commanded by an Armenian trader named Kosikh, representing in Central Asia the Moscow firm of Konshin and Co. Kosikh was already known at Merv to many Tekkes who had transacted business with him in the Askabad bazaar.

Alikhanoff played the part of clerk to Kosikh the trader, and also acted as interpreter. It was a great advantage to him in his expedition that he spoke the language of the Turcomans quite fluently. To assist him in his survey a cornet of the Cossacks, Sokoloff, was appointed, and was also disguised as a caravan clerk.

To prevent any possibility of a failure of the enterprise, the Russians decided that they would not ask the permission of the Merv Tekkes to visit them, but would pounce upon them unawares. Alikhanoff, England knows to her cost, is an expert in effecting surprises, and his audacity was never better displayed than in his caravan journey to Merv.

Quitting Askabad early in February, 1882, the caravan, consisting of a few camels escorted by half a dozen well-armed Turcoman horsemen, set out for Merv via Kahka and the Tejend oasis. The distance by this route is about 230 miles, and is divided into six marches. The distance from Merv to Herat is 240 miles.

Fazil Beg, the spy, went on to Merv beforehand to secure some guides for the expedition, and arrange with the pro-Russian party for the protection of the traders as far as he could. During the journey Alikhanoff made a thorough survey of the country, exploring parts unvisited by Mr. O'Donovan, and, entering Merv at night, encamped in the midst of the Tekkes, without anybody being aware of it except the chiefs in Russian pay.

The next morning, of course, there was a great hubbub at Merv. The people were not quite so staggered as when Mr. O'Donovan put in his sudden appearance among them, for many had become acquainted with the Russians in the interval; but they were more angry, and had not Alikhanoff possessed influential supporters among the chiefs, things would have fared badly with the caravan. At the least, they would have been expelled at once from the oasis.

As usual, a meeting of the khans and elders was convened the moment the presence of the Russians became known, and the latter were summoned to appear before it. The meeting took place in a large *kelrtka* or tent, to reach which the Russians had to pass through an "immense" crowd of sightseers. "Entering the kelrtka," says Alikhanoff, "Kosikh, extending to every one his hands, which were shaken very unwillingly, sat down, as befits a rich Russian merchant, side by side with Mahdum Kuli. I, as interpreter, sat on a felt at the entrance. The silence continued. Waiting some time for some one to speak, I decided to break it myself. I therefore commenced with something like the following harangue:

"'From the letters you have received, you doubtless know the aim of our journey. My master, Severin Beg, is a rich Russian merchant. He enjoys the greatest respect of our authorities, and hence they instructed him to give their *salaam* to the people of Merv. Deciding to establish commercial intercourse with you, Severin Beg has come here to find out, on the spot, whether he can buy and sell in your markets. The Russian Government fully sympathizes with this action, since it anticipates from it mutual advantages, so desirable for the friendly and peaceful relations of neighbors. Thus, the sole object of our journey here is trade, and we should like to know what your views are upon the point, and how you mean to regard it.''

Another prolonged silence, broken at last by an old man, who said:

"' Commerce is a good thing, but we fear to draw upon us the responsibility which will arise if any attack is made upon you by those bad men who exist among us, as everywhere. Go back to Askabad to negotiate with our delegates. Fix our relations, and when both people are united, trade as much as you like,' etc., of an equally evasive character.

"' I tell you we are traders,' I rejoined; 'it is not our affair to join or disunite peoples. For that, apply to the Russian Government, send it your envoys if you like. As regards us, there is nothing undetermined in our relations. The Russians are at peace with you. The Askabad bazaar is filled with traders from Merv. We did not see, therefore, any reason why we should not come here, and hence resolved to come. Give us a decided answer. Will you let us unpack and commence trade, or do you demand our return? But mind, I warn you beforehand that your action will be viewed in its proper light by General Rohrberg, if you close to Russians alone that route which is freely made use of by the rest of our neighbors, Bokharans, Khivans, Persians, and Afghans. Just think what your relations will be with a powerful neighbor if the authorities at Askabad reply to your conduct by refusing to allow a single Mervi to put his foot on Russian soil? Who will be the loser then?'

Again a profound silence, broken at last by a discussion of the chiefs as to whether delegates should be sent to Askabad or not.

" ' We don't value the trade of Merv so much as all that,' I said at last, ' we are not disposed to waste our time running backward and forward. If we go back this time without selling our goods, you won't see our faces any more. I should like to ask you to tell me whether you assemble and debate every time a caravan arrives, or only do this to the Russians?'

" ' No, we would not assemble thus,' replied an elder. ' If anybody were to fall upon the caravan of any other country, if they were to rob it before my eyes, I could not even wink my eyes. We are not afraid of them; but we don't want anything to happen to you, the merchants of the great Padishah.'' .

" ' The people are ready to obey us,' added Kara Kuli Khan; ' we have no doubts on that score. But there are not a few *kaltamans* in the oasis—robbers from whom we ourselves are not safe. They might fall on your packs and on you yourselves.'

" ' If we do not meet with any hostility on the part of the people,' I replied, ' we will answer for the rest. Our arms and our escort will keep the robbers in order.'

" Again a profound silence. Makdum Kuli exchanged significant glances with his neighbors.

" ' I have said all I have to say,' I continued; ' we will now await your answer. If it be the same as before, we shall prepare for the journey back to Askabad.'

" I felt sure that the previous answer would not be repeated.

" After another discussion Makdum Kuli said: ' Tell the trader, that we are only influenced by fears for his safety, otherwise, we have nothing against him, and he may stop here forever if he likes.'

" ' God forbid!' I replied. ' It will be quite enough to stop here two or three market days to see what your trade is.'

" ' In that case, here is our answer,' said Makdum Kuli. ' Let him remain here two or three market days, and afterward return to Askabad with the delegates.' ''

This was agreed upon, and the assembly broke up. Alikhanoff's account of the discussion throws a broad light upon his adroitness in managing Asiatics. He thoroughly understands their ways.

The Russians stayed a fortnight at Merv, during which Alikhanoff made as many friends as he could, and intrigued against those who were disposed to interfere with the accomplishment of his great aim. Disguised afresh as a Tekke, he availed himself of every opportunity to explore the oasis, and by stealing out at early dawn secured unobserved a survey of the fortress of Merv.

He himself was quite at home among the Tekkes, but Kosikh grew nervous after hearing that some of the people had been plotting against his life, and hastened the departure of the caravan. Alikhanoff took advantage of the return journey to survey another route between Askabad and Merv.

Shortly afterward, another Russian officer, a Mussulman, named Naserbegoff, who had accompanied Stolietoff to Cabul as topographer, was sent to Merv in disguise, and pushed on thence to the

Oxus. By this time the Tekkes had lost so much of their hostility to the Russians, that it was felt that an agent might be sent there openly. Lessar was selected for this mission, and passed through Merv to Khiva without exciting any animosity. In this manner Russia secured within a twelvemonth a survey of all the roads converging from the Turkestan and Transcaspian oasis upon Merv, and dispelled the disinclination of the people to receive Russian visitors.

Another success followed upon this. Alikhanoff, who had maintained close relations with Makdum Kuli, persuaded that chief to throw in his lot with Russia, and proceed to Moscow to witness the Czar's coronation. His submission was considered a great gain for Russia. He had been the soul of the defense of Geok Tepé, and the authorities at Askabad had always feared that he might repeat that terrible resistance at Merv. His departure from the oasis left the people without a leader, and henceforward the Russians felt that they could afford to play a bolder game.

I saw Makdum Kuli several times at the Czar's coronation. He lodged with other Asiatics at a hotel opposite the rooms assigned to me by the Russian Government. The splendor of the Kremlin festivities thoroughly tamed him, and when he returned with the rest of the Turcomans to Askabad he was as little disposed to fight Russia any more as Cetewayo after his trip to London.

Knowing how great his personal influence at Merv had been, Alikhanoff induced him to pay a visit there on his return, to describe to his fellow-countrymen what the glories of Russia were like. His descriptions of the sight he had seen at Moscow exercised a most depressing effect upon the anti-Russian party, while at the same time the handsome Russian uniform he wore, and the account he gave of the favors conferred upon him by the Emperor, provoked a desire among other chiefs to make the acquaintance of such generous masters.

---

## CHAPTER II.

### THE SWOOP UPON MERV.

Russia, angry at our continued occupation of Egypt, resolves to seize the gates of Herat—Secret concentration of troops at points commanding Merv—Colonel Muratoff goes to the Tejend oasis "to return," but remains—Sudden appearance of Lieutenant Alikhanoff at Merv—The intrigues resulting in the acceptance of the Suzerainty of Russia—Russia promises to place only one officer in the oasis—Sudden advance of the Tejend force behind the Askabad deputation of chiefs—The Merv Tekkes hurriedly resist, but are defeated, and the Russians enter the fortress—Alikhanoff made governor of Merv.

JUST then the Egyptian question was exciting a good deal of attention. Our active interference in Soudan affairs had not yet begun, and during the lull preceding it a general European discussion was prevailing as to whether England should or should not evacuate Egypt. Russia had never concealed her opposition to our being there at all, and she therefore threw herself vigorously into the controversy.

To understand her feelings properly we must endeavor to examine things a little from her stand-point. Russia makes no secret that she is determined some day to have Constantinople. Her longing tor the Bosphorus is as great now as it ever was in her career. The most resolute opponent to her arms is England. Austria and Germany she believes may be " squared;" but up to now it has been impossible to buy off England. Still Russia has always nourished a hope that when matters reached a decisive stage, our acquiescence might be purchased by allowing or assisting us to annex Egypt. Cairo was the price to be paid for Constantinople.

I have no space to go fully into the details of this policy; but I have said enough to indicate that Russian statesmen could not be pleased at our occupying Egypt and offering them no compensation. We appropriated the power of Egypt; we assumed control of the Suez Canal; and still we as fiercely as ever refused to allow Russia to advance upon Constantinople.

I shall be told that Russia had no right to be angry at our occupation of Egypt, since we had no intention of annexing the country. In reply, I must ask that matters be again looked at from the Russian stand-point. Russian policy is dictated by the impressions and the feelings of Russian statesmen, not by the impressions of Englishmen. The general impression in Russia at the time was that England had virtually annexed Egypt, and that the fluctuations and contortions of Mr. Gladstone's policy masked a cut and dried plan for permanently retaining the country.

Anybody who has lived in the military states of Europe can easily understand how such an impression should have arisen. The statesmen of Russia, Germany, Austria and France usually formulate a policy long in advance of current events, and resolutely apply themselves to deliberately working it out. English statesmen, on the other hand, mostly live from hand to mouth. The occupation of Egypt was the result of no deep " design," using the term in the continental sense. England floundered into the Egyptian embroglio, and yet the errors of her statesmen did more to root her influence and authority in the country than the cleverest scheming could have done. Now, men who make events are apt to think that others make them also. Russia, at first disposed to treat Mr. Gladstone's disinterested policy as generously as that statesman's Liberal supporters, observed after a while that England benefited so largely by his blunders that she began to ascribe them to a deep and clever plan.

When England first sent troops to Egypt there were three great obstacles to a prolonged or permanent occupation of the country. In the first place, the English public generally were averse to it; in the second, the Egyptian people, it was thought, would never tolerate a foreign ruler; in the third, most politicians held that all the Great Powers would oppose it.

The first two obstacles had practically disappeared by the autumn of 1883. After the collapse of Arabi Pacha's army the whole of Egypt proper submitted without a struggle to English authority. Excluding the Soudan, the country proved amazingly easy to rule. The people, in short, appeared to be so utterly unable to do without their new masters that England began to look upon herself as marked out by Providence to control the country.

Of course she only meant to control it for a time, but to Russia, who had opposed any occupation at all, it was as obnoxious that she should remain in Egypt three, five, or fifteen years, as forever. What

England considered a troublesome burden, Russia regarded as a splendid acquisition—a grand dependency possessing all the elements of a second India. Our continued occupation, therefore, displeased her. Finding we were indisposed to evacuate the country at once, she decided she would establish a counterpoise in the East. She resolved to reopen the Central Asia Question.

The Emperor was perfectly aware that Merv was no counterbalance to Cairo, or Sarakhs to Alexandria; but what he had in view was the creation of a new base that would enable him to reopen in turn the Eastern Question on advantageous terms. Merv, if a " mere collection of mud huts," as the Duke of Argyll expressed it, was the stepping-stone to Herat, and at Herat he would be able to put the screw on England if her policy in Egypt continued to displease him.

I have been at pains to describe the influence the Egyptian Question had on the occupation of Merv, because, if it be clearly appreciated, the subsequent movement to the gates of Herat will be found to contain a larger amount of menace than is commonly imagined. The swoop upon Merv was no hap-hazard event. No local reason whatever provoked it. Russia was not forced to occupy Merv by any circumstance on the spot compelling her, against her wish, to violate her numerous assurances to this country. I believe that I am acquainted with everything that has been published in Russia— official or non-official—bearing upon the occupation of Merv. This published literature does not contain a single charge against the peo‧ ple of Merv, in excuse for the annexation.

Therefore, all that has been written in England by writers ignorant of the course of events in Russia, extenuating the annexation on the grounds of the difficulty of keeping the Merv Tekkes in order except by annexation, is theoretical nonsense. The Merv Tekkes were in excellent order at the time, so far as Russia was concerned. They had committed no outrages on Russia, and were committing none. It was as safe for Russian caravans to journey from Askabad to Khiva, across a desert which, anterior to the previous campaign, had been a prey to disorder, as to journey from Tashkent to Samarcand, or Tiflis to Baku. The Merv Tekkes scrupulously avoided attacking Russian subjects, and it was a matter of common notoriety that these man-stealers of the Asiatic steppes, finding their occupation as such gone, were becoming quiet, hard-working, industrious peasants.

It is true that there were small forays now and again against the Persians of the Atak oasis, a district stretching from the Russian frontier to Sarakhs; but they were a mere bagatelle compared with the great plundering expeditions the Tekkes twenty years previous had led in different directions, and Russia herself was indirectly responsible for them.

The Atak oasis was an integral part of Persia. The Shah's right to it was never questioned until Russia occupied Askabad. The Alieli and other Turcomans paid tribute regularly to the Shah's representatives, and appealed to them for help when they quarreled with the Tekkes of Merv. If that help was not always forthcoming, it did not demonstrate that the Atak was not part of Persia, for the people of the oasis were as much given to forays as the Tekkes, and, as often as not, were themselves the offenders.

To put an end to this condition of things, Persia prepared, after the occupation of Askabad, to exercise more stringent authority over the people of Atak. The Shah felt that, if he only kept them in order, and prevented them perpetrating small raids upon Merv, the people of Merv in turn, having no provocation for their forays, would suspend their outrages. The Persian authorities admitted that their Atak subjects provoked the raids, and one has only to refer to O'Donovan's book to see how exasperating they could be toward their Merv neighbours across the desert.

But I wish it to be clearly understood that, after all, these raids were very rare subsequent to the occupation of Askabad—say half a dozen times in the course of a season, and that only a few individuals participated in them. The Persian border from Askabad to Sarakhs was incomparably quieter than it had been in O'Donovan's time, and had the Shah's troops occupied two or three points in the oasis, the last vestiges of border turbulence would have disappeared. Russia allowed the troops to almost reach the district, and then delivered a sort of ultimatum for bidding them to enter it.

The English Government protested strongly against this. It demonstrated clearly enough the Shah's claim to the territory. It showed how great would be the benefit to the people of Atak and Merv if the frontier were properly administered. Russia refused to listen to any arguments. She would not occupy the district herself, and she would not allow Persia to do it. She kept open this tiny sore on the Persian frontier in order that if ever she wanted a pretext for occupying Merv one would be immediately forthcoming.*

Of course this was not the sole reason; there was another and greater one. The easy road from Askabad to Herat, *via* Old Sarakhs, runs through this Atak oasis. Had Russia let Persia assume definite control over it, the advance upon India would have been blocked. Russia could have only advanced with the permission of the Shah, or by violating his territory. This circumstance gave an importance to the Atak oasis out of all proportion to its intrinsic worth. It was, from the Russian stand-point, absolutely essential to Russia.

From what I have said, which, in common with the greater part of this book, is based on Russian information, it will be seen that there was no tribal turbulence on the Russian frontier at the time the swoop was made upon Merv; and that, as regards the Persian border, the old raids had dwindled down to petty pilferings, which could have been suppressed at any moment if the Emperor had allowed the Shah to keep his subjects under better control.

So insignificant were these pilferings, that Russia has never attempted to cite them as an excuse for the occupation of Merv. It is only a few English writers who have put forward the plea, and they have done so because they were ignorant of the true state of affairs on the Russo-Turcoman frontier in the autumn of 1883.

To me it has always appeared ridiculous, as well as unpatriotic, for Englishmen to invent pleas for Russia's aggressiveness based on

---

* The negotiations on the question of the Atak oasis will be found in Blue Book, Central Asia, No. 1, 1884.

mere theory, which Russia herself does not take the trouble, or is unable to put forward, in extenuation of her advances toward India. Tribal turbulence provoked the conquest of Geok Tepé, and Russia's contention on this score I have always defended. But tribal turbulence did not provoke the occupation of Merv, and those who fancy it did should just remember that Russia herself has never sought justification on these grounds.

Nor is the plea that Alikhanoff and Komaroff acted on their own responsibility any sounder. Russia herself has never advanced this excuse. It is only English writers who have done so, and done so without the slightest basis for their erronous assertion. I can prove this at a stroke.

In the spring of 1883 the garrison of Khiva, located at Fort Petro-Alexandrovsk, consisted of the 4th Regiment of Orenburg Cossacks, the 5th and 13th Turkestan line battalions, and the 6th battery of artillery. This was the strength of the garrison, according to the official report published in Russia early in the year, and it tallied, I have good grounds for believing, with the list in the possession of the military authorities at Simla, derived from non-Russian sources. In the autumn of 1883 the garrison was increased by the arrival of the 17th Turkestan line battalion from Samarcand.

I only knew of this last year, after the occupation of Merv was an accomplished fact. Every day I received from Russia the principal newspapers, including those of the Caucasus and Turkestan; and one morning, glancing through the *Moscow Gazette*, I saw that among the sufferers from a flood at Fort Petro-Alexandrovsk were the men of the 17th line battalion. Now this battalion belonged to the garrison of Samarcand, distant at least a month from Khiva, by the quickest possible means of conveyance—how, therefore, had it come to be shifted to the latter place, and for what reason?

This was explained in an equally casual manner a short time afterward. Writing from Fort Petro-Alexandrovsk to the same paper, a correspondent, signing himself Gospodin Tchursin, mentioned, among other things, the suicide of Lieutenant Bodisco, of this same 17th battalion, " who had been in a state of deep melancholy from the time, six months previous, when the battalion had been sent from Samarcand to Khiva, to be dispatched to Merv, and who had preferred blowing out his brains to accompanying it any further."

This 17th battalion, therefore, was sent to Khiva from Samarcand, in the autumn of 1883, to take part in the occupation of Merv. As soon as Alikhanoff induced the Merv Tekkes to submit, it marched from Khiva to Merv, *via* Tchardjui, on the Oxus, and now forms part of the regular garrison of the place. Bodisco, who was homesick, refused to accompany it any further, and committed suicide. The demonstration is clear, consequently, that Alikhanoff's swoop upon Merv was not a filibustering exploit, carried out by him and other frontier officials on their own personal responsibility. Alikhanoff and Komaroff were under the control of the Governor-General of the Caucasus, Prince Dondukoff-Korsakoff. The 17th line battalion, on the other hand, was under the control of General Tchernayeff, the Governor-General of Turkestan. The two ad-

ministrations are as widely distinct as the governments of India and
Canada. To secure the simultaneous action of the two administrations
in support of one another, the impulse must proceed from St. Petersburg. As a matter of fact, the 17th battalion was marched to Khiva
by the order of the Minister of War, and, to cut unnecessary argument short, the whole of the operations culminating in the occupation of Merv were directed by the authorities at the Russian capital.

It is well to bear in mind that although this stealthy movement of
troops in Turkestan was not known to the public of this country,
the military authorities in India were cognizant of it.   Through the
Hindoo traders arriving from Turkestan and other sources the Intelligence Branch was placed in possession of information, difficult
to disbelieve, that the Russians were moving toward the Afghan
and Turcoman territories.   The military authorities appealed to the
Marquis of Ripon to take timely precautions against this move, but
their warnings were pooh-poohed and their counsels disregarded.

While the Turkestan authorities were concentrating troops to take
part in the occupation of Merv, the officials of the Caucasus were
not idle.

In October our Minister telegraphed from Teheran that the
Governor of Askabad, General Komaroff, had sent a force to the
Tejend, and established a fort there.   The Tejend may be roughly
described as the midway oasis between Askabad and Merv.   It is
there that the Hari Rud or Tejend, the river watering Herat and
Sarakhs, buries itself in the Turcoman sands. Although larger than
the Merv oasis, it was practically unoccupied until after the fall of
Geok Tepé.   The Persians would not let the Mervis settle there, and
the Mervis would not let the Persians.   After Skobeleff took Geok
Tepé, General Kouropatkin pushed on to the place, and found there
several thousand fugitives.   These submitted, and either returned
home or settled down along the Tejend River, Russia promising to
protect them from the Persians.   As the Tejend oasis was a no
man's land before then, their submission conferred upon Russia, in
her opinion, a sort of right to the country.

From Askabad to the Tejend oasis is about 120 or 130 miles, the
road running along the Russian oasis of Akhal and Persian oasis of
Atak to Kahka, a large Atak settlement 80 miles from Askabad, and
then turning off at right angles across the plain to the Tejend, 50
miles to the north.   Readers of O'Donovan's book will remember
that the dashing Irishman made a halt on the banks of the Tejend.
He quitted the Persian frontier at Mehne, 53 miles to the east of
Kahka, and traversed the 50 miles to the Tejend in a night.   From
the Tejend to Merv the 80 or 90 miles' distance is usually done by
the Turcomans in a day or a day and a half.

After things had settled down in Central Asia, subsequent to the
English evacuation of Afghanistan, and the Russian annexation of
Askabad, a small Cossack force was periodically sent to the Tejend.
The excuse for this movement was that the new settlers there were
Russian subjects, and that Russia required a proper topographical
knowledge of the oasis.

At first the Merv Tekkes were extremely alarmed at the approach
of the Cossacks so close to their country, and assembled in thousands to bar the way across the plain to the Merv oasis.   But when,

time after time, the Cossacks returned without advancing beyond the Tejend, they grew less suspicious.   They were gradually lulled into a false security.   In this manner when, at length, the Russians sent a larger force than usual to the Tejend in the autumn of 1883, the Merv Tekkes went about their ordinary occupations, and made no preparations for defense.   They had at Merv a fortress far larger and stronger than the one at Geok Tepé Skobeleff had nearly broken his army to pieces in battling his way into, and, what was more, they had cannon; but, not imagining that the Russians had any immediate designs on their oasis, they undertook no measures of defense.

It is well to bear these facts in mind, because Russia is endeavoring to secure the Badgheis district of Afghanistan a pouncing position similar to the one on the Tejend.   Ak Robat is even closer to Herat than Kari Bent, on the Tejend, is to Merv.   Russia, in 1883, lulled the Mervis until she had got them completely off their guard, and then she pounced upon their stronghold, regardless of all her assurances to England.   In the same manner, if we let her retain the gates of Herat, she will wait until a favorable moment occurs, and then the key of India will be carried by a sudden *coup de main.*

The military movement in the direction of the Tejend did not escape notice in England.   A discussion arose as to whether the expedition to the Tejend did not constitute a violation of Russia's assurance not to advance beyond the limits of the last annexation.  Thereupon the *Journal de St. Petersbourg* which must surely have told more fibs in its time than any existing newspaper, published an indignant denial of the reports in circulation.   The movement of troops to the Tejend was not an "expedition;" it was simply a reconnaissance.   It then drew a fine distinction between the two expressions.   An "expedition," said the organ of the Russian Foreign Office, "always goes and stops, but a reconnaissance always returns!"

Considering that Russia had already mapped every inch of the Tejend region, and knew through the explorations of Alikhanoff, Lessar, Nasirbegoff, and others, the whole of the surrounding country, the necessity for even a "reconnaissance" was not very apparent; above all, a reconnaissance by a force, which, according to our Minister at Teheran, comprised 1,000 infantry, 500 cavalry, and 10 guns.

Our embassador at St. Petersburg, Sir Edward Thornton, was thereupon instructed to make inquiries at the Russian Foreign Office.   In reply he wrote: "His Excellency, M. Vlangaly, said that he was *no' aware* of any force having been sent in that direction,[*] but he was not surprised at learning it.   He said that on the occasion of the raid which had been made about two months ago into Persian territory by Turcoman raiders, when they carried off a number of cattle, etc., and, as he believed, some men, the Persian

---

[*] The conversation took place Jan. 2, 1884.   Yet the organ of the Foreign Office had said, Nov. 10, 1883: "Il y eu en effet une reconnaissance faite sur le Tejend (there has been, in fact, a reconnaissance made on the Tejend)," so that he could not have been totally unaware of it.   However, his memory brightened up when Sir Edward gave him to understand that we knew what was going on, although he refused to impart any information, or admit more than was squeezed out of him by our embassador.

Government had appealed to the Imperial Government to use their influence for the recovery of their cattle, etc., which had been taken. Instructions had consequently been sent to the commander of the forces at Askabad to do his best to meet the wishes of the Persian Government. M. Vlangaly supposed that it had been impossible to do so without the use of force, and that a small detachment had consequently been dispatched for that purpose; but his Excellency doubted whether it could be nearly so large as I had mentioned, or could he answer my inquiry as to the particular direction which the force in question would take."

It must not be supposed that this raid was a very large one, simply because the Shah had appealed to Russia for redress, or that the Shah could not have himself secured reparation if he had applied direct to the Merv Tekkes. The simple fact is, that Russia had not only prevented the Shah from administering the Atak frontier, but had also severed the close relations previously existing between Merv and Teheran.

As is well known to readers of Oriental history, Merv was once a dependency of Persia. After the Russian movement toward India commenced from the Caspian, British diplomacy for years did its utmost to get the Shah to establish a Persian protectorate over Merv, and the Merv Tekkes, to acknowledge it. It was a very foolish policy, because, to put the matter briefly and forcibly, English statesmen tried to place the desert lion under the control of the Persian jackass. A far more sensible plan was that suggested by Colonel Valentine Baker when he visited the Perso-Turcoman frontier in 1873. This was, to place the Mervis under the Afghans.

Readers of Vambery's delightful "Travels is Central Asia" can not have forgotten the amazing instances he gives of Persian cowardice. A dozen or more Persians, attacked by two or three Turcomans would not only throw down their arms and beg for mercy, but also ask for the cords and bind each other prisoners, without making the slightest attempt at resistance. The Afghans, on the contrary, were quite a different people to deal with. The Merv Tekkes always admitted that they were braver men than themselves.

The notion of passing under the rule of the Ameer was therefore not distasteful to them. After Valentine Baker's return the Government sent on a special mission to the Perso-Turcoman frontier Major Napier, son of Lord Napier of Magdala. This was what he reported home:

"The occupation of Merv by an aggressive power will open the way to further extensions of influence on what has always been the weak side of Afghanistan, the side of Herat. As to the reasons underlying the evident desire of the Tekkes for an Afghan alliance, there is a very general impression abroad that an alliance with Afghanistan—the Afghans are their co-religionists—means an alliance with England. I received" (from the various Tekke chiefs he saw) "abundant proof of their desire for a direct connection with us, and I believe that they might be turned into a peaceful, honest, and prosperous community, and would prove a real strength to the border and to the empire."

Not long afterward General Sir Charles MacGregor paid a visit to Sarakhs and Herat, and also advocated the inclosure of Merv within the political limits of Afghanistan, but his words fell flat on the ears of the authorities. England persisted in weaving her ropes of sand for binding Merv to Persia, and only left off when Russia sharply declared after the annexation of Askabad that she would not tolerate any more efforts on the part of the Shah to establish his influence there.

LIEUTENANT ALIKHANOFF.

An intimation, in effect, was conveyed to Persia that if she wished to carry on diplomatic intercourse with Merv it must be done through the medium of the Askabad authorities. Previously the Shah and the Mervis had settled their quarrels themselves, by the short and summary process of retaliation one against the other, varied by occasional truces, during which they exchanged prisoners and hostages. The Shah had now to appeal to Komaroff. In this manner Russia secured for herself a pretext for meddling with the affairs of Merv. If the Mervis failed to raid against Russia the latter could always harass them by bringing them to book for their raids on Persia—raids, be it remembered, largely occasioned because Russia would not allow the Shah to put his frontier districts in order, and keep his own subjects from raiding against Merv.

Now this particular raid mentioned by Vlangaly having occurred, and Persia having appealed to Komaroff for redress, all that the latter needed to do was to send a message to Merv, when reparation would have been at once forthcoming. The attack the previous year on the Parfenoff surveying party was a far grosser outrage, yet the tribe disavowed it at once, on receipt of Russia's demand for the offenders. In the interval Russia's influence had become immensely more powerful at Merv. This is avowed by Lessar and others. But Russia needed a pretext, and this not to justify herself in the eyes of the Tekkes, but to blind England as to her intentions on the Tejend. She did not wish her projected *coup de main* to be frustrated by the action of England.

On the spot Russia did not trouble herself about the pretext at all. When the force proceeded to the Tejend no ultimatum was sent to Merv, nor was any attempt made to settle the matter promptly. As a matter of fact, the sufferers had already done that themselves. They had seized some camels belonging to the Mervis, and squared their own loss by inflicting another on their neighbors.

Undeterred by England, therefore, Russia was able to consolidate her position on the Tejend, and await events. By the end of the year everything was ready for the swoop. All that was now needed was some complication that would divert England's gaze, and minimize the force of her indignation on finding the annexation of Merv an accomplished fact.

The occasion was found early in 1884. The long pent storm in the Soudan had burst, and the Government were seriously embarrassed. Baker Pasha had just gone to the East Soudan to relieve Sinkat, and General Gordon was on the point of starting for Khartoum. The belief was general that our troubles were only just commencing in the Soudan, and in no country was this impression stronger than in Russia.

Events, consequently, were ripe for the swoop. The decisive moment, for which the Russian Government had deliberately prepared by assembling forces on the Turkestan and Transcaspian sides of Merv, had at length arrived. The signal was given for delivering the blow.

Acting on the orders transmitted to him by General Komaroff, Alikhanoff started off for Merv, accompanied by a few horsemen and the hero of Geok Teppé, Makdum Kuli Khan. Arrived there he put up for the night at the tent of Yousouf Khan, one of the four chiefs of Merv, and brother to Makdum Kuli. Yousouf, like many of the leading men, had already been bought over to Russia.

The next morning a public meeting was convened, and Alikhanoff read out to the people Komaroff's ultimatum. Immediate submission was demanded, and, to enforce his threats, Alikhanoff pointed to the Tejend and announced the force established there to be simply the vanguard of a greater army then advancing toward the oasis.

That the submission was not a purely voluntary one is proved by the following passage occurring in the Russian *Graphic* (*Vse-mirnaya Illustratsia*), from the pen of Gospodin Krijanovsky, a Russian officer of Askabad, who sent that paper a sketch showing the submission of the Merv chiefs in General Komaroff's drawing-room. He says: "General Komaroff, wishing to take advantage of the impression which had been produced on the Tekkes by the dispatch of a detachment of our troops to the Tejend, ordered Lieutenant Alikhanoff and Major Makdum Kuli Khan to proceed to Merv, and invite the Mervis to beg for mercy and become Russian subjects." The *Svet*, which is edited by the brother of Komaroff, supports this by its disclosure of the threats which Alikhanoff used with reference to the Tejend column being the vanguard of an advancing army.

Having already created a strong pro-Russian party by his intrigues, Alikhanoff experienced very little difficulty in persuading the people to accept the suzerainty of Russia. His arguments were no doubt strongly backed by the renegade, Makdum Kuli, who was probably compelled to dilate on the glories of Moscow, where, among other things, he had witnessed, within a few paces of Lord Wolseley, the feeding of half a million people and the review of 100,000 troops.

According to reports prevalent in Russia, Alikhanoff secured acquiescence all the more readily by wrapping up his terms in tissue paper. He repudiated any intention of occupying the country with a large garrison. All that Russia would do if they submitted would be to send a governor with two or three assistants, and things would go on the same as before.

England was treated in a similar fashion. When M. de Giers officially informed our embassador of the submission of Merv, Feb. 15, he intimated that, in accepting it, the Emperor would simply send "an officer" to administer the government of that region. He added that "this officer would perhaps be accompanied by an escort of Turcomans!"

The solitary Russian officer proved to be as expansive as the famous four and a half battalions sent to Khiva a decade earlier. "To give an idea of the Khivan Expedition," said Count Schouvaloff to Earl Granville, January 8th, 1873, "it was sufficient to say that it would consist of four and a half battalions." In reality Russia sent to Khiva 53 companies of infantry, 25 sotnyas of Cossacks, 54 guns, 6 mortars, 2 mitrailleuses, 5 rocket divisions, and 19,200 camels, with a complement of about 14,000 men.

At the bidding of Alikhanoff, the principal chiefs and elders signed a parchment deed he had brought with him, and selected a deputation to proceed to Askabad. On the way the party was joined by Colonel Muratoff, the commander of the Tejend force, and arrived at Askabad on the 6th of February, two days after the annihilation of Baker Pasha's army at Tokar. The next morning, at 11 o'clock, the four chiefs and twenty-four notables took the oath of allegiance to the White Tsar in General Komaroff's drawing-room.

When the ceremony was over, Komaroff made a short speech to them, in which he declared that now they had made their submission to Russia, they would find the White Tsar a valiant protector of their interests. "To prove this to you," he said, "I telegraphed this morning to Teheran, demanding that the Persians should give up to you the hundred camels they took the other day, and I have just received a message from the Shah acceding to my request."*

Not a word was said about the cattle taken from the Persians, which had served Russia as a diplomatic pretext for assembling Muratoff's force on the Tejend. That was conveniently consigned to oblivion.

Russia, in a word, having made use of a Persian grievance to steal the independence of Merv, rounded on the Shah the moment the theft was accomplished, and treated him in turn as a delinquent. One can easily understand the Mervis exclaiming, " How great a ruler is this Russian general! He has only got to send a message to the Shah, and the sovereign of Persia submits at once to his dictation!"

Several days were spent in feasting, and then came the *dénouement.* General Komaroff decided to proceed to Merv, and this was made the pretext for dispatching more troops—as a guard of honor!—to the Tejend. Arrived there, the whole available force was set in motion behind the returning deputation, and Fort Kari Bent being only three marches from Merv, the Russian army was already close to the oasis before its approach was known.

The elders were the first to arrive. They confirmed the reports that the Russian army was advancing, and asked the people to take out water to the troops. A tumult arose. A strong party, headed by Kajjar Khan, protested against the invasion, and threatened to kill anybody who obeyed the elders' request. They then applied themselves to the discussion of the best means of repelling the Russian advance.

The Merv oasis is not very large, and it is surrounded on all sides by barren plain or desert. Retreat from it was practically impossible. The Russians controlled three sides, and the Sáriks—bitter enemies of the Tekkes—the fourth. To defend themselves against an invader the Tekkes had built an immense clay-ramparted inclosure, capable of accommodating the entire population with their herds and cattle. But there was no time to assemble the people inside it before the Russians arrived. The Mervis felt that they had no course open to them but to surrender.

The reports current in Russia that Alikhanoff tricked the people into submission by promising that no garrison should be installed, are strongly supported by this tumult. If the army had been expected, the so-called " anti-Russian party " would have organized resistance and made a stand somewhere. As it was, nothing whatever was done, and when the intelligence arrived that the Russians were already close at hand, the only thing the Mervis could do was to go out on horseback, and fire a few ineffectual shots into the column by way of a protest.

While the excitement was still prevailing, Alikahnoff entered the oasis with a *sotnya* of Cossacks and endeavored to allay it. The attitude of the people, however, was so defiant that he thought it prudent to take the advice of his Merv friends and fall back upon

* Krivanovsky's narrative.

the Russian army, then camping for the night twelve miles distant from Merv.*

After dark Kajjar Khan, with several thousand horsemen, made an onslaught on the Russian camp, but was repelled with heavy loss. The next morning (March 16) the Russians marched early and occupied the fortress without serious resistance. Lessar says that altogether there were three fights or "skirmishes." The Russian loss, he adds, was "one man." Kajjar Khan fled to Afghanistan.

The fortress was far too large to afford security to the Russian force. General Komaroff, therefore, impressed several thousand Mervis at once, and compelled them to build, under the supervision of his officers, a regular fort on the European principle. The completion of this sealed the fate of Merv.

In reward for his successful swoop Alikhanoff received the rank of major, and all his decorations; he was also made Governor of Merv. Makdum Kuli was rewarded by being appointed head of the Tejend oasis. Komaroff received the Order of the White Eagle, his district was raised to the rank of a province equal to that of Turkestan, and he himself was made governor-general.

To further add to his importance, he was assigned permission to carry on diplomatic intercourse direct with the neighboring states of Persia and Afghanistan. In other words, if he wished to intrigue with the Ameer without resorting to the instrumentality of the Foreign Office at St. Petersburg, he was at liberty to do so. Lessar was appointed his diplomatic agent for this purpose.

The news of the occupation of Merv excited a storm of indignation in England. At first, the artful manner in which the Russian Government represented the annexation as a "voluntary submission" provoked a few excuses. It was said that as the people of Merv themselves had asked to become Russian subjects the Emperor was, to a certain extent, justified in relieving himself of the burden of his assurances to England. "After all," it was a happy ending to the Turcoman question, and Russia, having got Merv and rounded off her frontier, would trouble us no more.

Before a week was over, however, Komaroff's brother had let the cat out of the bag. The editor of the *Svet*, himself a military officer, was so proud of the cleverness displayed by his brother in accomplishing the swoop, that he published an account of the operations on the Tejend, and the audicious threats of Alikhanoff that had brought about the submission of Merv.

From this account sprung the impression that Alikhanoff and Komaroff had acted as filibusters, and forced the hands of their Government, but the facts I have given demonstrate this impression to be totally wrong. It is an impression which has never prevailed one moment in Russia. There is nothing in the *Svet* narrative to justify its existence, and the account I have given of the concentration of troops in Khiva disposes of the notion completely.

To be short and plain, Alikhanoff and Komaroff simply acted according to the instructions telegraphed to them to Askabad, and no

* Some of these particulars are taken from the narrative of a Turcoman eyewitness, published in an Indian paper. They curiously tally with Russian reports.

more anticipated the desires, or forced the hand of their Government, than Lord Wolseley did when he invaded Egypt and conquered Arabi Pasha.  If Alikhanoff's diplomacy at Merv was shady, it was not a whit darker in hue than the diplomacy exercised by the Russian Minister for Foreign Affairs at St. Petersburg.

The annexation of Merv was deliberately planned by the Russian Government, and carried out in strict accordance with its orders. The *coup de main* was totally unprovoked by the Tekkes; it was done in violation of a whole series of solemn assurances to England and the blow was struck in a treacherous and cowardly manner, dishonorable to a nation that had produced such a hard-hitting, fair-fighting hero as Skobeleff.

When Russia annexed Askabad, I defended her action against the whole English Press.  When the excitment took place over the Atrek boundary convention with Persia in 1882, I issued a map to Parliament and the Press, based on the new treaty with the Shah, showing that Russia had done no evil.  In my various writings on Central Asia I have always justified her policy when I thought it fair, and have never hesitated to condemn the policy of England when I considered it stupid or selfish.

I can fairly claim, therefore, that when I denounced the annexation of Merv, on the news becoming known in this country last year, I did so without any avowed animus as a Russophobe.  I felt that the Emperor had broken his solemn promises, and the promises of Alexander II., without the slightest measure of justification.  Nothing has been published in Russia since to shake this conviction, while the facts that have come to light have only strengthened what I believe to be a fair and impartial view of the transaction.

There had been two widely distinct and clearly opposed views of the Russian advance, among members of the House of Commons, up to the time of the annexation of Merv.  The debate that took place when the news became known, was the first that found the two sides united as to the necessity for disregarding further assurances, and opposing a firm and unsevered front to Russian aggression.

According to the *Newcastle Daily Chronicle*, this unanimity was, to a certain extent, due to a pamphlet I circulated in the House among all the members just before the debate began, giving an account of Merv and the results which I believed would inevitably spring from the annexation.  In that pamphlet, which served as a handbook to the debate, I drew particular attention to the open character of the country lying between Merv and Herat, and I printed in large type this warning:*

"That the annexation of Merv, being inevitably attended with the incorporation of the Sarik Turcomans, will extend Russian rule up the Murghab to Penjdeh, at the foot of the Paropamisus, to within 140 miles of the Key of India. England, at the same time, being still posted at Quetta, 514 miles from Herat."*

---

* Five hundred copies of the pamphlet, "The Russian Annexation of Merv," with three maps, and a frontispiece illustrative of Merv, were struck off in twenty-four hours.  There being no time to post them, they were distributed in the members' lobby.  "Soon after the House assembled, half the persons in the lobby might have been seen with the orange pamphlet in their hands.  As the House filled, a demand arose for copies among the minor members who had

How I came to predict so correctly the second Russian advance, from Merv to the gates of Herat, can be best described in another chapter.

---

## CHAPTER III

### THE ADVANCE TO THE GATES OF HERAT

General Petrusevitch's secret survey of Afghanistan in 1878—His suggestion that Russia, after occupying Merv, should insert a wedge between Herat and Meshed—Concentration of troops at Merv—General Komaroff seizes Old Sarakhs—Alikhanoff's intrigues with the Sarik Turcomans—His attempt on Penjdeh—Lumsden finds the Russians advancing up the Hari Rud, and posted at Pul-i-Khatun—Russia displays the dispatch of General Zelenoi in order to push further toward Herat—Occupation of the Zulfikar Pass, Ak Robat, and Pul-i-khisti.

WHEN, in the early part of 1881, exciting telegrams were arriving every day from Russia, describing Skobeleff's terrible conflict with the Tekkes at Geok Tepé, it may be remembered that one of those messages recorded the death of a general, who fell in a night assault upon the fortress. The name of that general was Petrusevitch. So far as I am aware, he was the first to suggest the idea of thrusting the Turcoman wedge from Merv to the Paropamisus mountains, and under cover of it securing the gates of Herat.

Petrusevitch was quite a different type of officer from Alikhanoff or Komaroff. Honest, truthful, averse to intrigue, and devoted to his duty; he was, in one word, a representative in actual life of that ideal of an Indian administrator which is commonly held in this country. The district he governed in the Caucasus for many years was a model of good order, and he was so deeply respected by the hill tribes, although not a fighting man, that when he fell at Geok Tepé they sent a deputation to the scene of the conflict, to beg Skobeleff the body of the deceased general, to bury it in their midst.

Petrusevitch was first dispatched to the Transcaspian region in 1874, and there is every reason to believe that he pushed his explorations into Afghanistan as far south of Herat as Seistan. In subsequent years he undertook other journeys along the Perso-Turcoman frontier, from the Caspian to Sarakhs, and in 1879, just before he received the appointment of Governor of Krasnovodsk, in succession to the defeated general, Lomakin, he penned an exhaustive report upon the Turcomans.

In this report he traced, in dealing with the Turcoman tribes of

---

not received them, and Mr. Marvin, who was in the lobby, dispatched a special messenger for a hundred more. In this manner, when the debate actually did come off, nearly everybody used it as a hand-book, and there can be hardly a doubt that it secured a very important effect upon the speeches, observable in the unanimity with which the members of both parties insisted on the necessity of trusting Russia no more, and the imperative need of firm and decisive measures on the part of the Government. During the debate, Mr. Marvin sat under the gallery, watching the effect of his pamphlet."—*Newcastle Chronicle*, February 28, 1884. The pamphlet was translated into German; and in India an eminent military officer, well known for his patriotic interest in the Central Asia Question, published, at his own cost, an edition at Bombay, and distributed copies throughout the Peninsula.

the Merv-Herat region, the Afghan and Persian frontiers in such a fashion as to leave open the gap which Russia has just occupied. Up to then it had been accepted both in England and Russia that the Afghan dominions extended from the Oxus to Sarakhs. Petrusevitch was the first to bulge back the frontier to the hills at the rear of Penjdeh, less than one hundred miles from Herat.

A copy of this report reached me from the Caucasus, and I made it the backbone of a work I was then preparing on the Turcomans. To me this hint or claim of Petrusevitch's seemed so ominous, that I drew a series of maps to illustrate the menace it conveyed to the security of Meshed and Herat.

Respecting his contention I said, in translating his words in full: "Particular attention should be paid to this passage by political writers. The attempt to force a recognition of a 'no man's land' between Meshed and Herat is, in reality, nothing more than an effort to extend the Turcoman region wedge-fashion between Persia and Afghanistan. _Russia, in occupying Merv, will inevitably claim the right to extend her power along this wedge also._ The conquest of Akhal extends her rule to Gyaoors—_the conquest of Merv will extend it to Penjdeh._"*

My work was published in 1881, and was purchased for the Government Departments in London and Simla. It can not, therefore, be said that the Government were unaware as to the serious results that would inevitably attend an occupation of Merv. To prevent all possibility of Russia advancing her present claims to Penjdeh and other gates of Herat, I urged that the Afghan frontier from Sarakhs to the Oxus should be organized without delay, and the gap indicated by Petrusevitch closed up before the Russians occupied Merv.

"Do what we can," I wrote, "we can never prevent the inevitable junction of the Russian and English frontiers in Asia. It would be difficult to do so, even with Russia's help. It is impossible without it. . . . If we wait till Russia enters Merv and posts Cossacks on the Paropamisus ridge, we shall have to accept, at the dictation of Russia, _her_ delimitation of the two empires, with the dishonorable drawback of having to cede the best of the India-menacing points to her—as the power in possession. Since the junction of the frontiers of the two empires must some day take place; since we know that on the occasion of the next great war between the two powers, Russia will attempt to strike at our empire in India; since we have evidence beyond dispute that there exists an easy road of invasion—is it too much to demand of the rulers of our empire that they arrange at once our border line in Central Asia? Is it too much to ask of thinking Englishmen that they shall individually do their utmost to preserve the empire from the madness of masterly inactivity?"

These words were written four years ago, but they produced no effect upon the Government. The impression prevailed that a great mountain barrier, 10,000 or 15,000 feet high, intervened between

---

* "Merv, the Queen of the World; and the Scourge of the Man-Stealing Turcomans." 450 pp., 11 maps. London: W. H. Allen & Co., 1881.

Merv and Herat, and that even when the Russians secured the former they would fail to have easy access to the latter.

Yet our ablest authorities had done their utmost to disabuse the minds of English statesmen of this disastrous error. Colonel Valentine Baker, on his return from the Perso-Turcoman frontier in 1873, had pointed out the ease with which a military movement could take place from Merv to Herat, up the valley of the Murghab.

"Merv," he said, "with its water communication nearly complete, lies only 240 miles from Herat, to which place it is the key. There can be no doubt that Merv is the natural outwork of Herat, with the advantage of water supply all the way between the two cities. Strategically, the Russian occupation of Merv would be, so to say, the formation of a lodgment on the glacis of Herat. It would place Herat completely at her mercy."

General Sir Charles MacGregor, chief of Roberts's staff at Candahar, and since then Quartermaster General of India, went closer to the Paropamisus ridge than Baker, penetrating in 1875 to within a few miles of Herat. What he wrote on his return was plain enough for any man to understand.

"A Russian authority, M. Tchichacheff," he observed in his *Khorassan*, "declares that Herat would be in no danger even if the Russians were in possession of Merv, because the road between these places lies over an impracticable range of mountains. I must, however, take leave to deny this statement in the most decided manner. I have been to the Herat valley, and have followed a considerable part of one of the roads to Merv, and I have made the most careful inquiries from people on the spot who were in the constant habit of riding over the rest of the distance. Yet there is so little impression of difficulty on my mind, that I would undertake to drive a mail coach from Merv to Herat by this road."

Still, English statesmen persisted in placing faith in great mountain barriers between Merv and Herat, and the Duke of Argyll, pooh-poohing Valentine Baker and MacGregor, cracked an elephantine joke by telling the public not to be "Mervous" about the fate of "a few mud huts." The Russians were welcome to Merv: when they got there they would be as far off India as ever.

Much of the bad statesmanship of the time, as I have already said, must be ascribed to the confusion existing in the minds of English politicians with regard to the double character of the Russian advance. There were two movements, from bases thousands of miles apart, running in the direction of India; one from Orenburg and Tashkent over a colossal range, 15,000 to 20,000 feet high; the other, from the Caspian over a plain and occasional hills. English politicians, Conservative as well as Liberal, mixed up one with another. Because the Turkestan line of advance was difficult, therefore the Caspian line of advance was more or less impracticable. One has only to read the Candahar debates to see how widespread this confusion was, and how little even talented Conservative politicians realized the real bearings of the new advance. Lord Salisbury was the only one who thoroughly grasped the facts of the situation.

The "Paropamisus bugbear" was finally disposed of in 1882, when Lessar explored the country from Sarakhs to Herat, and discovered the mountain range, 15,000 feet high, to be simply a ridge of hills, with passes only 900 feet above the surrounding locality. Across those passes from Sarakhs to Herat, and from Merv to Herat, he found that a vehicle could be driven without the slightest difficulty. Practically, there was no barrier at all intervening between Herat and Merv.

Lassar's discovery provoked great attention on the part of experts in this country, but nothing was done by the Government to fill in the gap to which Petrusevitch had given prominence.* The Marquis of Ripon, ignoring General Roberts's appeal that he should do so, gave the Ameer a subsidy and some arms, but this was all. No steps appear to have been taken to induce the Ameer to bulge out his Herati administration to the proportions indicated on English official maps, until after the occupation of Merv.

We thus see that the Government were well warned as to the danger the gates of Herat would run of being captured after the conquest of Merv, and upon the Marquis of Ripon and the Gladstone cabinet must rest the blame of having refused to take any steps to protect them. From the time Petrusevitch gave England the hint of what Russia would do with the Turcoman wedge, up to the actual seizure of Merv, was a clear interval of three years. That precious period was allowed to pass away without the slightest effort to organize the Afghan frontier north of Herat.

Consequently, when Komaroff occupied Merv in force on the 16th of March, 1884, and turned his face toward Herat, the country lay practically open to him to the very walls of the Key of India.

It was the consciousness of this that rendered the annexation of such serious import to me. I knew that Petrusevitch's suggestion that Russia should advance from Merv to the gates of Herat had been borne well in mind by the Russian Government, and I was well aware that the Marquis of Ripon had done nothing to anticipate this movement. It was for this reason that, in issuing my new pamphlet, I printed in capital letters the warning that "The annexation of Merv, being inevitably attended with the incorporation of the Sarak Turcomans, will extend Russian rule to Penjdeh, or to within 140 miles of the Key of India."

The warning had but very slight effect upon the Government. Four or five months later the Ameer occupied Penjdeh, but—if the *Times* is to be believed—entirely on his own initiative. Considering the importance the Government suddenly attached to the gates of Herat after the Russians had occupied them, would it not have been more sensible to have forestalled the aggressors? There was no one to prevent the Afghans occupying Ak Robat, Zulfikar, and Pul-i-Khatum months and months before the advance from Merv took place; and, had the Government given the Russian menace adequate heed, they would have advised the Ameer to have done so instead of leaving him to act upon his own initiative.

To prevent England adopting a course of this kind the Russian Government embarked upon a series of negotiations, which dawdled

---

* A full account of Lessar's explorations, together with Alikhanoff's narrative of his journey in disguise to Merv, was published in "The Russians at Merv and Herat" in the spring of 1883 by the writer. Most of the twenty-two illustrations accompanying it are from the talented pencil of Alikhanoff.

on through the summer and enabled it to consolidate its position at Merv.

As might be expected, when Komaroff occupied Merv in March, the feeling of the people for a time ran very strong against the Russians. The least impulse from without would have set the Turcomans in revolt  This was the proper period for the Ameer to have moved down the Hari Rud and Murghab to the limits assigned him on the Russian official maps—Sarakhs and Imam Bukash—and the question of delimitation could have been settled afterward.

GENERAL ALEXANDER KOMAROFF.

Such a move could have been easily accomplished in a week or ten days. On neither river was there a man to oppose this advance, and it could have been effected without spilling a drop of blood or wasting a single rupee. Under the supervision of two or three English officers, the occupation of the Badgheis territory could have been carried out in such a manner that Russia would have been left without the slightest cause for just complaint.

The Turcomans of Merv would not have resented the approximation of the Afghans, and if Russia had sought to oppose the step, we could have responded to her threats by an intimation of the ease with which she could be turned out of the district she had just annexed, contrary to the feeling of the inhabitants.

But a manly and statesmanlike policy was hardly to be expected from a Cabinet which by its vacillation had involved us in so many difficulties. In India it is an open secret that Sir Frederick Roberts, Sir Charles MacGregor, and other eminent generals, appealed in the strongest terms to the Marquis of Ripon to secure the gates of Herat before the Russians had time to advance from Merv. The Viceroy refused to take any action in the matter.

Thus the sore and hostile feeling of the Tekkes was allowed to die away, and Komaroff was left unchecked to consolidate his hold upon the newly conquered country.

As soon as possible, the troops that had been concentrated in Khiva were dispatched to Merv. The Caucasus Regiment of Kuban Cossacks was also dispatched from the Caucasus to re-enforce the garrison. In May Prince Dondukoff-Korsakoff, the Governor-General of the Caucasus, himself set out to visit Merv. The prince traveled through Turkmenia in a calash, and it may be interesting to mention, that if, when he quitted 'Askabad, he had turned his course toward India, instead of toward Merv, he could have traveled all the way in that same calash to the Chaman outposts of Quetta.

Advantage was taken of the presence of the prince to accept the submission of the Sarik Turcomans dwelling at Youletan. This place naturally belongs to the Merv oasis, and the annexation of the few thousand Sarik families dwelling there, consequently, was almost a matter of course.

The case was different with Old Sarakhs, which was formally annexed by General Komaroff immediately afterward. Sarakhs, like Merv, had been dubbed by military men the key of Herat. To a force advancing from Turkestan to Herat Merv is the key; to a force advancing from the Caspian the key is Sarakhs. The two points are about 80 miles apart; Merv is 240 miles from Herat, and Sarakhs 202. Whatever may be the views of party politicians, the leading military men of England and Russia have long regarded Sarakhs and Merv as the two keys of Herat—the two points where troops could concentrate and rest before maing their final advance upon the Key of India.

Russia, through her diplomatic organs, intimated her intention of annexing Old Sarakhs in advance of the actual occupation. The news excited interest second only to that provoked by the seizure of Merv. At this juncture, Lord Fitzmaurice exhibited a lamentable amount of flippant ignorance in replying to questions put to him in the House of Commons. First, he did not appear to know that there was such a place as Old Sarakhs, although it had been marked on Russian maps for years. Then, when the Foreign Office discovered the whereabouts of Old Sarakhs, the excuse was gratuitously put forward on behalf of Russia that the point annexed was of very little importance. It was only a heap of ruins!

What I said at the time, in contending with this view, will bear repetition now.* " From a strategical point of view, the one town is as good a base as another. To put the matter plainly, if London

---

* *Morning Post* Leader, May 26, 1884.

were Herat, and North and South Woolwich Old and New Sarakhs respectively, the menace to the city would be just as great from the Woolwich on the one side of the river as from the Woolwich on the other. The circumstance of Old Sarakhs having been the first site occupied in ancient times, would appear to indicate that it is the best spot in the locality for a town. New Sarakhs was simply erected on the west side of the river by the Persians (who besieged and destroyed Old Sarakhs fifty years ago), because the river formed a protection against the Turcomans of Merv. Hence, although the Russians are taking possession of a lot of ruins, they have presumably secured the best site for an administrative center, where they will be able to draw away all the importance from the dirty, straggling Persian town lying across the water to the west.''

The error current at the moment was the ascribing of the strategical significance of Sarakhs to the site of the actual town instead of to the locality generally. There is a danger that this may be repeated in the case of Herat also, and what I said in continuation may therefore be appropriately repeated:

'' Even had the Russians annexed the new town, they would have had to build their own cantonments, as at Tashkent; hence it is an altogether immaterial point whether they have got Old or New Sarakhs. They have secured all that they wanted, and all that English strategists sought to deprive them of—a lodgment in the Sarakhs district—and from this new base they will be only 202 miles, or five marches, distant from Herat. Of these two hundred and two miles, 130 are uninhabited; consequently, the Russians can roam over the plain to Kusan, 70 miles from Herat, without being checked by a single Persian, Turcoman, or Afghan. Lord Fitzmaurice seems to imagine that English diplomacy has done enough in preserving New Sarakhs from Russia, or, rather, that Russia has been considerate enough in taking the old site—for English diplomacy preserves nothing. Never was there a greater error. So little is Persian Sarakhs important as a fortified point, so little advantage has it over half a dozen other spots in the same locality, that General MacGregor recommended that the Persians should shift the fort some miles from the present spot.

'' Hence it is no gain whatever to England that Russia should have spared New Sarakhs. If she be allowed to settle down on the old site, she might just as well be allowed to have the new town as well. Seven hundred Persian soldiers are no menace to Russia, and directly she establishes herself at Old Sarakhs the Persian fort will become as valueless as the Martello towers on the English coast. On this account, looking at the matter from a broad, comprehensive, military and political point of view, and ignoring the barleycorn measurements of English diplomacy, the occupation of Old Sarakhs by Russia possesses all the significance, and embodies all the menace, that has been ascribed to the act by the ablest generals of England and Russia.''

Apart from its military significance, Old Sarakhs was important politically, owing to the circumstance that the Afghan frontier was supposed to touch the Persian border near this point. For years the Persians had controlled the district, and Old Sarakhs was looked upon as indisputably theirs. The Afghan frontier was regarded as commencing alongside it.

By the submission of Youletan and Old Sarakhs, Russia secured the whole of the region of Central Asia lying outside the Afghan frontier marked on Russian and English official maps. She obtained thereby an excellent frontier, well rounded off, and there was absolutely no reason why she should have stepped across it into Afghanistan. England was angry that she should have seized Merv and Sarakhs in violation of her promises, but still, now that Central Asia was blotted out, the public were ready to condone the past. They admitted that there were plenty of excellent reasons to justify the annexation of the steppes and khanates of Central Asia, and so long as the Afghan frontier was respected, they were prepared to overlook all that had been done to bring the Cossack cordon flush with the Ameer's dominions.

On this account, England received with satisfaction the announcement that Sir Peter Lumsden had been appointed to proceed to Sarakhs to define the Russo-Afghan frontier to the Oxus. In order that the work might be well done, the Government assigned the envoy a brilliant staff of assistants.

Sir Peter Lumsden was an officer of thirty-seven years' standing. He had seen service in various Indian frontier expeditions, the Central Indian campaign, under General R. Napier, and in the China war. He served with several expeditions against the frontier tribes between 1852 and 1856; was present as deputy quartermaster-general at the action of Punjhao in April, 1852; at Nowadund and other operations in the Renanzi valley in May, 1852; against the Bori Afridis in 1853; at Shah Mooseh Kheyl against the Meranzi tribe in April, 1855; against Bussy Khilut Alum in 1855; and the Meranzi and Kooroon expedition in 1856 (for which he received the special thanks of the Local and Supreme Governments). He was a member of the special military commission to Afghanistan in 1857-58, and again received the thanks of the Supreme Government, and was awarded a medal with clasp. He accompanied the expedition to China in 1860, and was present at the actions of Singho and Janchow, the assault and capture of the Taku forts, and the advance on Pekin, in connection with which operations he was mentioned in the dispatches, received a medal with two clasps, and obtained the brevet of major.. His latest active service was with the Bhotan field force in 1865, where he gained an additional clasp. From the foregoing summary of his career it will be seen that the commissioner possessed a considerable experience of Afghanistan and frontier affairs. He was also a member of the Indian Council.

In India the appointment provoked expressions of disappointment. The press, almost without exception, had selected General Sir Charles MacGregor for the task. This gallant and distinguished officer, the Skobeleff of India, possessed special qualifications for the mission. He had seen as much fighting service as Lumsden, and while the active military operations of the latter had terminated in 1860, MacGregor had participated in warfare so recently as 1879–81, acting as chief of the staff to General Roberts in Afghanistan. His reputation, therefore, stood high in Russia.

I say " therefore," because, while for our Afghan war as a whole

Russia entertains a contempt, Roberts's operations have always been singled out for special admiration. Skobeleff, and all of Skobeleff's set, were never tired of extolling the march from Cabul to Candahar. " It was a splendid march," said Skobeleff to me. " It was a grand operation of war," said Grodekoff. When I attended Skobeleff's funeral, I was repeatedly questioned about the march by his officers, and Roberts's name was never mentioned without respect and admiration.

Skobeleff always thought that he should some day lead an army against India His opponent in that case, he believed, would be Roberts. Being a great man, in every sense of the term, and not a mere military wasp, like our arch-hater General Soboleff, he took a generous interest in the fortunes of his Indian rival, and I have every reason to believe that this generosity was reciprocated. I can say, at least, that the feeling was prevalent among Roberts's lieutenants. Shortly after Skobeleff's death, Sir Charles MacGregor, in expressing to me his regret at his untimely end, said that he admired the brilliant young Russian general so much, that he had been anxious to undertake a journey to Europe solely and expressly for the purpose of making his acquaintance.

Besides being Roberts's ablest lieutenant, MacGregor was the hero of an exploit which should endear him to every patriotic Englishman. In 1875, having just finished for the Indian Government an elaborate gazetteer of Afghanistan and Central Asia, which revealed the many serious gaps that existed in our knowledge of that region, he set out, at his own cost and risk, to make a survey without precedent in modern times. Riding from the Persian Gulf, he made his way to Herat, then worked round to Sarakhs, afterward pushed along the Turcoman frontier to the Caspian; and when this 3,000 miles' ride was done, he quietly traveled on to the Caucasus and South Russia, and effected a survey of the Russian base also. Had he not been foolishly ordered home by the Government, he meant to have surveyed the country just seized by Russia, from Herat to Merv, and in that case the Paropamisus bugbear would have been exploded long before the Afghan war, and the evacuation of Candahar rendered impossible.

After this grand survey, for which, I may add, he was snubbed instead of being thanked by the authorities, he explored Beluchistan, fought alongside Roberts, and was then made head of the Intelligence Branch and Quartermaster-General of India. In India it was a matter of notoriety that MacGregor had studied the Central Asian Question more thoroughly than any military man living, and having a keen perception of good strategical points, it was felt that he would have secured for Afghanistan the strongest possible frontier. Hence, when the Government selected Lumsden, a comparatively unknown man, there was a cry of bitter disappointment in India. The Government, it was said, was going to patch up the Afghan frontier anyhow, as they had patched up everything else.

As I do not know the actual reasons that impelled the Government to choose Lumsden and reject MacGregor, I shold be sorry to condemn the selection. I have always had a warm admiration for Mac Gregor, which has been repeatedly expressed in my works, and I considered him the right man for the task. But the Government having, from reasons of their own, selected Sir Peter Lumsden, it would have been unpatriotic and ungenerous to have caviled at the appointment.

Before Sir Peter Lumsden left for the frontier, I had the pleasure of a long conversation with him on Central Asian affairs generally. In order that it should be free and unrestricted, it was agreed that the discussion should be confidential. I am, therefore, precluded from going into details, but I may state that I was thoroughly pleased with the Commissioner's clear appreciation of the issues at stake, and his determination to safeguard English interests. There were no traces of Russophobia in his talk, and I felt that if Russia were as really desirous of harmoniously arranging the frontier as she made out, there could be no possible hitch between him and his Muscovite colleague.

I may point out one very important advantage that has resulted from sending Lumsden to the frontier instead of MacGregor. The former had published nothing on Russia that intriguers in this country could use against him, while the latter had expressed opinions in his books which, if detached and garbled, could have been made to convict him of Russophobia. Had the Skobeleff of India been therefore sent, all the complications that subsequently arose on the frontier would have been laid to his door, as a hater of Russia. This possibility was prevented by sending Lumsden, and not being able to blacken that prudent officer, the Russians have had to pile all the blame on the Afghans and his subordinates.

Very luckily, as events turned out, the Government provided the envoy with a splendid staff. Let me describe some of the members. Among those who proceeded from England, or joined the General on the way to Sarakhs, were Major Napier, Colonel Patrick Stewart, Mr. Condie Stephen, and Captain Barrow. Napier, as I have already said, had been to the Perso-Turcoman frontier in 1874. He was there repeatedly in subsequent years on behalf of the Government, and thus was not only familiar with the region, but was also intimate with the leading Turcoman chiefs, and knew thoroughly the recent history of the contested country.

Colonel Patrick Stewart was an Indian officer who had done a very patriotic thing in 1880. At that time Skobeleff was massing his forces for the purpose, it was believed, of marching to Merv; and, in spite of the excitement provoked in this country thereby, the Government resolutely refused to send anybody to the frontier to find out what he was actually doing. Whereupon, Colonel Patrick Stewart, being at home on furlough, quietly proceeded via Turkey, at his own expense, to the East, and, having by a circuitous route reached Ispahan, doffed his European garb, and departed disguised as an Armenian horse-dealer. Speaking Armenian well, and being thoroughly acquainted with Eastern habits, Stewart preserved his disguise so well, that when, after twenty-six days' riding, he reached the frontier, close to Geok Tepé, and took a shop in the bazaar, he lived alongside Mr. O'Donovan three weeks without the latter being aware that he was an Englishman.

At length the Government got to know that he was stalking Skobeleff, and, to conciliate Russia, ordered him home; but they were so pleased with his conduct that they sent him out soon after

to Khaf, a Persian town near Herat, where he could act as English
agent for Western Afghanistan and watch Russia's operations without exposing England to the danger that might arise from having a
political resident installed in the key of India.

Stewart was acquainted with the Russian language, and so also
was Captain Barrow, another Indian officer of great ability, who,
after studying it at the Staff College, had gone to Russia and buried

MAJOR-GENERAL SIR PETER STARK LUMSDEN, K.C.B., C.S.L.

COMMANDER OF THE AFGHAN BOUNDARY COMMISSION.

himself for three months at Moscow to render his knowledge more
perfect. There is little doubt that a distinguished career lies before
him. The official Russian scholar, however, was Mr. Condie
Stephen, Second Secretary to the Legation at Teheran. He had
acquired the language so perfectly while attached to the Embassy at
St. Petersburg, that he had been able to render into English a
splendidly spirited translation of Lermantoff's great poem, "The
Demon." He likewise had traveled along the Sarakhs frontier, and
had been grossly insulted by a Russian official in 1882 in making

his way to the Atak oasis, for which M. de Giers had made a lame and inadequate apology. Napier, Stewart, and Condie Stephen were thus three frontier experts, equal in knowledge and experience to any Russia could dispatch to confront them. Russia was perfectly aware of this. She therefore made no attempt to send any at all, and, instead, shot Gospodin Lessar into London.

The escort and the surveying staff were furnished by India, and had to march through Afghanistan to Herat, and join Sir Peter Lumsden on the Perso-Afghan frontier. The contingent was composed of the following persons:

Chief Political Officer: Lieutenant-colonel J. West Ridgeway. Political Officers: Captain E. L. Durand, Captain C. E. Yate, Mr. W. K. Merk, Captain de Scessoi. Survey Officers: Major J. Hill, R.E.; Captain St. G. Gore, R.E.; Lieutenant the Hon. M. G. Talbot, R.E. Intelligence Department: Captain P. J. Maitland, Bombay Staff Corps; Captain W. Peacock, R.E. Naturalists: Dr. J. E. T. Aitchison, C.I.E. Medical Officers: Dr. C. Owen, C.I.E.; Dr. Charles. Native Attachés: Sirdar Mahomed Aslam Khan, Rissaldar Baha-ud-kin Khan, Rissaldar Major Mahomed Hussain Khan, Sirdar Sher Ahmed Khan.

Colonel Ridgeway, the officer in charge, was a man of great experience. He received his military training in the 98th Regiment, and was appointed to the political service fifteen years ago by Lord Mayo. During the Afghan war he acted as political officer to Sir Frederick Roberts, and took part in all his military operations. At the close of the campaign he was made Foreign Under-Secretary to the Government of India. In this manner he was intimately acquainted with the outer politics of India, and knew thoroughly the views of the Government.

Captain Durand was a son of the hero Sir Henry Durand, and for several years had been acting as political agent attached to the ex-Ameer Yakoob Khan, the ruler who connived at Cavagnari's murder at Cabul. Captain Yate had been political agent at Kelat-i-ghilzai during the Afghan war, and had been besieged there by the enemy. Merk was a wonderful linguist, and was noted for his skill in dealing with hill tribes. Scessoi was a Danish officer, who had once served in the Shah's army. Maitland and Talbot, Gore and Talbot, were Intelligence and Survey officers, noted for their pluck and capacity. The whole of the officers were picked men, and there was not one who had not participated more or less in hard fighting.

As regards the native members, they were all gentlemen of distinguished character and antecedents, and most of them were Afghans. Sirdar Mahomed Aslam Khan was a brother of the British agent at Cabul, and had charge of the local tribal levies of the Khyber. Rissalder Major Mahomed Hussain Khan had been employed for years on various delicate political missions. Rissalder Major Baha-ud-din Khan had served in every Indian campaign for thirty years, and was Sir Frederick Roberts's faithful henchman at Sherpur and Candahar. Sirdar Sher Ahmed Khan was a cousin of the Ameer and a son of the present Afghan Governor of Candahar, and had served as Ridgeway's assistant at Cabul. These native colleagues of the English "politicals" were thus not only most of them old personal friends and fellow-workers of the latter, but were also closely connected with the Ameer's officials at Cabul and Candahar. This was an immense advantage.

But this was not all. The Afghan Governor of Herat, the Naib-el-Hakmut Mahomed Sarwar Khan, was likewise an old friend of Ridgeway's. The mission was thus certain of a warm reception at Herat. Some troublesome tribes had to be passed at one section of the road (a very small and insignificant section), but every assistance was to be expected from the Ameer's officials.

To protect it against those tribes and any troubles that might arise on the Turcoman frontier, the mission was furnished with an escort composed of 200 men, splendidly mounted, of the 11th Bengal Lancers (better known as " Probyn's Horse ") and 250 bayonets of the 20th Punjab Infantry, than which no native regiment in the service contains men of finer physique and bearing. Major Ironside Bax was placed in command.

A correspondent who accompanied the mission says of these Indian troops, "The infantry were almost all light-hearted, cheery Afreedees of the Khyber Pass. They walk with extraordinary rapidity, and are big men. Their march is as quick as the ordinary pace of the cavalry; they are fine, high-spirited, free-spoken men, who cheer to the pipes' tunes as they march, and they come in at a swinging pace, with pipes playing, on each camping ground. The cavalry, Sikhs and Rajputs, are also splendid men, possessing excellent spirits, and are well equipped for the journey."

As usual, there were a large number of followers, and these swelled the total to 35 Europeans, and 1,300 natives. The transport consisted of 1,300 camels and 400 mules.

To avoid any chance of complications, the mission was ordered to proceed to Herat, not by the direct Candahar road, but by a more circuitous route through country comparatively unpopulated, and consequently free from fanatics.

Quitting Quetta on the 22d September, the party reached Herat on November 17th, having traversed over 700 miles,* at the average rate of eighteen miles a day, with relatively little hardship, and without any unpleasantness to speak of with the natives. The march was attended with a very important discovery. A route which had been hitherto treated as almost impracticable, was found to be available for the advance of a large army.

In other words, if the Russians penetrated to Herat by the easy roads Lessar had discovered, and we allowed them to remain there, they would be able with very little difficulty to advance into the heart of Afghanistan by the route opened up by Ridgeway's party. Hence the discovery of the practicability of the Nushki route for a large force rendered Herat all the more significant as the Key of India.

Arrived at Herat, Ridgeway was received in the heartiest manner by the Afghan Governor. "The two," says an eye-witness, "shook each other warmly by the hands. The Naib was in the best of humor; his full jovial face, of an olive tint, had a merry look, and his large soft eyes beamed a genial welcome. He looked such a Governor as he was reported to be—mild in his rule, and in

---

* 767 from Quetta to Kusan.

his acts showing good sense and practical justice. The good spirits of the Naib appeared to have affected the soldiers and irregular troops. They performed the exercises which we could see they thought would please us most. They were very anxious to win our opinion, and there was something very *naïve* in the manner in which they tried to gain it. After the Naib and Colonel Ridgeway had shaken hands, the Afghan infantry were put in fours and marched by companies in front of the mission, with the cavalry in the rear; with each movement the bugles—sweet sounds they were, too—sounded. As the troops marched by, the buglers began to play a lively martial air with a French ring. The little we heard of the bugle march was most effective. Many of the men wore woolly hats, which gave them a swaggering look. They were warmly clad and a large number had Sniders. The cavalry were well equipped and capable of going anywhere."

Another officer present says: "The artillery, consisting of mountain guns, marched past first. The guns appeared to be in good order. The cavalry were rather mounted infantry, and, so far as dress and horse accoutrements, they were perfectly equipped and were much admired by our officers. The irregular horse were better mounted, having larger horses, and had a gallant appearance. They rode by in a free easy pace, moving as if carefully trained. The officers were of many types, but the one who attracted our attention most was a captain, who wore a felt hat, which, if not disrespectful, I should call a billycock hat with a stiff rim and a gold-colored spike on the top. The other portions of the captain's dress were equally original and displayed much character. He had an Irish-American look, which was exaggerated by a chin tuft, for the captain shaved his cheeks. It was a much-disputed point whether the captain was an Irishman or not. I think he was not; but what do ye faithful of Hind say to this? The captain had a bulldog, and an excellent one, that ran at his heels and followed him at the side of his Herat regiment. And all this under the shade of Sheik Abdulla Ansari in the Herat valley! It only shows in another way that the Afghans are not all the intolerant fanatics they are supposed to be in England."

Between 2,000 and 3,000 troops mustered on the ground, and their march past was an event of the highest political significance. For the first time, after two generations of war, the Afghans passed in review before and saluted a British officer.

While the Afghans and the Indian contingent were fraternizing in sight of Herat, Sir Peter Lumsden was hastening to join them from Sarakhs. On the 19th of November, after a journey of 1,000 miles from Resht, on the Caspian, he joined Ridgeway's party at Kusan, 70 miles west of Herat, close to the Persian frontier, greatly to the relief of the Afghan Governor, for already events had occurred which had occasioned him deep anxiety.

Without waiting for the English and Russian frontier commissions to arrive upon the spot, General Komaroff had occupied Puli-Khatun, on the Hari Rud, and Alikhanoff was advancing up the Murghab. The gates of Herat were in danger.

It has been said that the Afghans provoked this advance by seizing Penjdeh, but there are one or two facts that will effectually

clear the ground of this contention. Penjdeh was occupied by the
Afghans in June or July, 1884. Lumsden left London in September. The occupation of Penjdeh had been announced in English
papers a long time before he left, and had been officially admitted
by the English Government. There was no secret whatever about
it. Why did not the Russian Government raise and settle the question before Lumsden left England? They had already selected
their commissioner, General Zelenoi,* and there was no reason why
he should not have arrived at Sarakhs in advance of Sir Peter
Lumsden. Instead of which they kept him back on various pre-
texts, and when ours began to approach the frontier from Teheran,
they pushed on their troops to Pul-i-Khatun, and endeavored to
carry Penjdeh by a *coup de main*.

Why the Russians should have made this dash at the gates of
Herat is capable of simple explanation.

We have seen that for some time after their seizure of Merv their
position at Merv was unsafe. It was in March when they effected
their swoop; it was in May that Youletan submitted—the Afghans
occupied Penjdeh late in June or early in July. Writing from Merv
in May a correspondent of the Tiflis *Kavkaz* stated that there
was still a considerable amount of discontent in the Tekke oasis.
Until this feeling subsided more, it was hardly safe to make a fresh
advance.

Still, Alikhanoff was not a man to rest inactive. The moment
the Sariks of Youletan submitted, he commenced intrigues with the
Sariks of Penjdeh. As I have already stated, Youletan is geographically part of the Merv oasis. The 4,000 Sarik families dwelling there consequently had always been on good terms with the
Merv Tekkes, and the fortunes of the two consequently traveled together. But Penjdeh is 80 miles distant from Youletan, and the
interval is an interval of desert. The fertile ground lies behind
Penjdeh toward Herat. Thus, geographically, Penjdeh is to Herat
what Youletan is to Merv, and the 8,000 Sarik families dwelling
there had not only paid tribute to the Ameer for years, but were the
fiercest enemies of the Merv Tekkes.† In this manner the submission of the Youletan Sariks in no wise carried with it the submission of the Sariks of Penjdeh. Had Alikhanoff advanced at once up
the Murghab, the Afghan Sariks would have doubtless resisted his
attempts to annex them.

Aware of this, Alikhanoff sought to buy them over. He sent
agents to Penjdeh to endeavor to persuade the people to declare for
Russia. Reports of this reaching the Afghan Governor of Herat,
he marched a small force to the place, and, with the perfect concurrence of the inhabitants, erected a fort at Ak Tepe to protect
them from Alikhanoff.

Considering the treacherous trick Alikhanoff had played ðn the
people of Merv, and which was better known to the surrounding

* It was erroneously stated, shortly after Lumsden left, that Russia had insulted England by appointing Alikhanoff as the frontier commissioner. There
was no ground for this statement. Sir Peter Lumsden himself told me, before
his departure, that Zelenoi had been chosen for the post.

† See Petrusevitch's report in "Merv, the Queen of the World," and Lessar's
accounts of his own explorations, in the "Russians at Merv."

people than to this country, was there anything aggressive or un-warrantable in this? To my view, it was an unostentatious measure of defense of the most legitimate character, and no more carried with it any menace to the security of Merv than the English occu-pation of Cairo in 1881 interfered with the interests of Timbuctoo. Russia was chagrined at the failure of her intrigues at Penjdeh, but she masked her anger for the moment. She allowed two months to pass, apparently acquiescing in the occupation of Penjdeh, and at any rate refraining from the projected swoop upon the other gates of the Key of India. She refrained, partly because she wanted to make her Merv base safer, but mainly because she believed that the Indian contingent would never traverse Afghanistan without a com-plication of some kind with the natives.

It may be remembered that just before the departure of Ridge-way, frequent reports reached India of the presence of Russian se-cret agents at Cabul. How far these were true it is difficult to say. One thing, however, is certain. Russian officers in disguise have unquestionably visited Cabul since we installed Abdurrahman as Ameer,[*] and as their presence was attended by the receipt of similar reports in India, it is not improbable that some were there again last year. At any rate Russia believed for a long time that the Ameer would refuse to allow the Indian mission to pass through his do-minions and when his permission was given they relied upon the treachery of his officials and the hostility of the people to prevent it ever reaching Herat. When these expectations failed to be real-ized, decisive action was decided upon. Moving 40 miles south of Old Sarakhs, where he had established 200 infantry and several hundred Turcoman horse, General Komaroff placed a Cossack out-post at Pul-i-Khatun.

This marked the beginning of the Russian advance from the Merv-Sarakhs bases upon the gates of the Key of India.

Lumsden first heard of the movement at Meshed. Proceeding to Pul-i-Khatun he found the Cossacks established there, and pushing on to Sarakhs (Nov. 8) obtained a promise from Komaroff that there should not be any further advance, pending the settlement of the frontier question by their respective governments. Alikhanoff was with Komaroff at the time, and rode right through the English camp one day without taking any notice of the Commissioner. This insult caused a great talk at Sarakhs. Directly Lumsden left Sarakhs Alikhanoff set off for Merv, and, taking with him several hundred horsemen, pushed up to the Murghab, and tried to capture Penjdeh.

The Afghans, however, were again equal to the occasion. The moment Yaluntush Khan, Governor of Penjdeh, heard of the ad-vance, he sent a message to Ghaus-nd-din, Governor of Bala Murgh-hab (on the road to Herat), and the latter, with laudable prompti-tude and energy, started off, accompanied by all his cavalry, with a foot soldier behind each trooper. At the same time he dispatched a courier to Herat for reinforcements. Arrived at Penjdeh, he found Alikhanoff posted at Pul-i-khisti, a few miles distant. To him he

* See narrative of Samuel Gourovitch, interpreter to the Venkhovsky secret mission of 1882, in " The Region of Eternal Fire."

at once sent a message, asking him if he meant to fight or not, frankly informing him that he was ready for the conflict. Ali-khanoff, disappointed at being outwitted, returned a savage and insulting letter to the Afghan general, and withdrew. Had he not done so, the Afghans were so excited that they would have probably attacked him. According to a correspondent, their blood was up, and they were most anxious to fight.

Russia, having now cast off the veil, no longer attempted concealment. Her Cossacks were pushed forward as fast as they could, and occupied in swift succession the Zulfikar Pass, Ak Robat, and other avenues to Herat.

It has been said that Afghan restlessness provoked this advance. This I am able to deny on unquestionable authority. The Ameer's right to Penjdeh will be dealt with directly. The annexation of that place, as I have demonstrated, provoked no feeling in Russia, and evoked no immediate reciprocal move. The real Afghan advance that Russia puts forward as excusing her own advance, subsequent to Sir Peter Lumsden's arrival, was the advance from Penjdeh to Sariyazi–a short distance to the south. But what are the facts of the case? There was no occupation of Sariyazi in the annexationist sense of the term. Hearing that the Russians had advanced from Sarakhs to Pul-i-Khatun, and tried to cut off some Afghan horsemen, led by an Afghan official, proceeding to join Sir Peter Lumsden, the plucky Governor of Bala Murghab I have just described thought that the Russians meant war. They were advancing up the Hari Rud toward Herat; perhaps they were also moving up the parallel River Murghab in the same direction. He was in charge of the Murghab line of defense. It was his duty to bar the road to Herat. He, therefore like a good soldier, sent out an Afghan picket to Sariyazi, so that Fort Ak Tepe at Penjdeh might know in time of the advance of the enemy. Sariyazi was not on Merv soil, whether it was Afghan or not. Thanks to this picket, when Ali-khanoff did advance with his horsemen, his approach was signaled in time, and his *coup de main* frustrated.

Thus there was no restlessness, no aggression on the part of the Afghans. They set an example of good order and good faith to the Russians, which would have done credit to any civilized power.

---

# CHAPTER IV.

## THE QUESTION OF THE BOUNDARIES.

Russia's claim to the gates of Herat—The original agreement between England and Russia as to the Afghan frontier—The disputed territory—Discrepancies in English official maps—The frontier generally recognized by the two countries—Skobeleff's map of Merv and Herat, showing what Russia regarded as the frontier in 1881—Lessar's mission to London—The Russian claims impartially considered.

Russia's claim to cave in the Afghan frontier appears to have been first officially made shortly after the annexation of Merv, when the Russian General Staff issued a sixpenny map, showing the Sarakhs-Oxus border bulged in to within 50 miles of Herat. This, I believe, was the first official intimation that Russia had adopted Petrusevitch's idea.

I issued a fac-simile copy of the map, which found its way into the principal English newspapers, and the Russian claim was indignantly denounced. Still, none the less, the impression prevailed that the map was only a feeler. Russia had demanded a good deal, in the hope of getting at least some small concession. The English Government had a reputation for yielding to pressure. When Sir Peter Lumsden left England, it was generally believed by those behind the scenes that England had surrendered Pul-i-Khatun. I can not say how far this report was true. I simply record what impression prevailed at the time.

On this account, when the news was telegaphed from Meshed that the Russians had occupied Pul-i-Khatun, it fell to a certain extent flat. Russia had greedily taken in advance what had been promised her after the frontier was settled, and the move was simply another instance of her barbarous manners. It was never imagined that she claimed all the Afghan territory to the gates of Herat.

At length, after a deal of uneasiness and indignation had been expressed at Zelenoi's unaccountable tardiness in proceeding to the Afghan frontier, it became suddenly known in London that Russia had pushed up to Penjdeh. While the excitement was still in progress, the Russian Government unexpectedly dispatched the ex-railway engineer, Lessar, to London to expound its claims. The demands of Russia then became public.

An elaborate account of these demands, with the Russian arguments in favor, and the English arguments against them, would only tire the reader. Let me, therefore, put the case as shortly, but as plainly, as possible.

In 1872 elaborate negotiations took place between the Russian and English Governments with regard to the north-east Afghan frontier. The Russian advance then lay through Turkestan, and the Orenburg Cossacks had reached the Oxus. It was necessary, therefore, to define in some manner the Oxus side of the Ameer's dominions. After long negotiations this was accomplished, and as since there has been no infringement of that frontier, we may dismiss it without further remark.

Respecting the north-west border, from the Oxus to Persia, the settlement was not so satisfactory, nor could it be so. The Russians even then had designs upon Merv, which we wished to treat as part of Afghanistan, and they, therefore desired to draw the line south of it. By assenting to this, it was thought at the time we should surrender the Tekhe oasis to Russia. Ultimately the matter was left open.

Considering that the Turcoman barrier was still unbroken, that Herat was in a turbulent condition, and that the Merv region seethed with disorder, this course of action on the part of the two Governments can not be severely criticised. They had fixed the starting-point of the line at Khoja Saleh, on the Oxus, which no Russian has since contested, and if the term, "Persian frontier," or "Hari Rud," be not a precise termination, we must bear in mind that the gaze of the two Governments and the two nations was not fixed upon the end of the line, so much as upon the middle. There was no quarreling about the termination of the line, only whether the line itself should curve north or curve south. If it curved north

Merv was included in Afghanistan; if south, it was excluded from it. As time passed on, the English and Russian Governments decided to treat it as excluded from Afghanistan although this country still reserved its right to watch the fortunes of the Tekkes.

As regards the terminal point, discrepancies undoubtedly exist on the official maps of the two countries, but an overwhelming majority of both fix it at Sarakhs, and it is particularly noteworthy that cartographical harmony was arrived at during the period immediately preceding the advance upon Merv. The map that Skobeleff used in his Turcoman war of 1881 traced the frontier from Khoja Saleh to Sarakhs identically with Arrowsmith's map of 1875, published in Rawlinson's "England and Russia in the East"—that English official text-book of the early phases of the Central Asian question—and this line was practically admitted by Russian diplomacy.

We may say, in short, that after Russia began to push seriously toward Merv, the Sarakhs-Khoja-Saleh line was tacitly adopted by the statesmen of the two countries as the north-west frontier of Afghanistan. It is well that there should be no misconception about this. Russia knew that England considered this line the Afghan frontier, and, therefore, when her statesmen gave assurance after assurance that they would not violate the integrity of Afghanistan, they were aware that England accepted those assurances in good faith as implying that the Sarakhs-Khoja-Saleh boundary would be respected.

Nay, Russian statesmen themselves by their words fixed the line, and showed that they recognized Sarakhs as the terminal point. Let me quote one instance. Early in 1882, a year before the swoop on Merv took place, England endeavored to persuade Russia to come to some settlement about the Perso-Turcoman frontier, stretching from near Askabad to Sarakhs. Russia in reply said, in effect, that it was no business of England's, but, if she liked, she would discuss the settlement of the Afghan boundary beyond, from Sarakhs to Khoja Saleh.

This recognition of the Sarakhs line was made during a special interview between Prince Lobanoff and Earl Granville on February 22, 1882. Directly the Russian Embassador was gone, Earl Granville wrote to Sir Edward Thornton as follows: "Prince Lobanoff said he had now received the reply of his Government. They acknowledged the continued validity of the agreement formerly entered into by Prince Gortschakoff, by which Afghanistan was admitted to be beyond the sphere of Russian influence. That agreement was, however, as I had said, incomplete; and they were ready to supplement it by a settlement of the frontier of Afghanistan from the point where it had been left undefined " (*i.e.*, the Oxus at Khoja Saleh) " *as far as Sarakhs.*" Thus the Russian Embassador in London treated Sarakhs as the ending point. Five weeks later M. de Giers discussed the whole subject with Sir Edward Thornton, when the Russian statesman stated positively that " Russia had no intention of advancing toward Merv or Sarakhs, or occupying any territory beyond what was already in her possession." At the end of the dispatch Sir Edward Thornton observes: " M. de Giers added that, with a view to preventing disturbances on the borders of Afghanistan, he considered it to be of great importance that the boundary of that country *from Khoja Saleh to the Persian frontier in the neighborhood of Sarakhs* should be formally and definitely laid down, and that he had instructed Prince Lobanoff to endeavor to induce her Majesty's Government to agree to the adoption of measures for that purpose.''*

Thus Russian diplomatists, as well as the official military map-makers, regarded the Afghan frontier as running from Khoja Saleh to Sarakhs, and the only point really undetermined by diplomacy was, where it crossed the Murghab River; but here, again, as Russian diplomatists followed their military map-makers as regards the two terminal points, it was a fair assumption that they followed them also in regard to the Murghab section. When English statesmen asked the statesmen os Russia for assurances, and the latter gave the solemn word of the Emperor that Afghanistan should be respected, those military maps, English and Russian, were, in almost every instance, and probably in all, lying on the tables or placed on the walls of the rooms where those assurances were given. To say, therefore, that Russian statesmen did not have the Sarakhs-Khoja-Saleh line in view, and in their minds, when they made those assurances, is to say that they were simply playing the part of blackleg lawyers, or Jesuits of the darkest hue.

Now this line not only includes Penjdeh, which is a good forty miles to the south of it, and Sariyazi, which is at least twenty, but also every point claimed or occupied by Russia. The Ameer, in occupying Penjdeh, simply occupied what Russian maps showed to be in his dominions. On the other hand, when Komaroff, many weeks later, occupied Pul-i-Khatun, 39 miles from Sarakhs; he occupied what Russian maps excluded from Turkmenia and also placed in Afghanistan. He violated, in short, the integrity of the territory of the Ameer. And the further he subsequently advanced, to Zulfikar and Ak Robat, the more he violated that integrity. In one plain word, he invaded Afghanistan. He crossed the line which Russian statesmen, in giving their assurances, had always treated as the boundary of the Ameer's dominions. Had Skobeleff marched to Merv in 1881, his movements would have been regulated by that line, for it was marked on the map which he used at the seat of war, and which is now in my possession. It bears the imprint of the Russian General Staff, 1881 (copies of it exist at the Foreign Office), and it was given me by General Grodekoff, the chief of his staff at Geok Tepé, in 1882.

The occupation of Penjdeh by the Ameer having preceded by a considerable time the Russian annexation of Pul-i-Khatun, let me deal with it first. In starting, I would point out that while one or two Russian maps anterior to 1881 show discrepancies in crossing the Murghab, they all of them unanimously assign Penjdeh to Afghanistan. Nor is this remarkable. Before the Sariks occupied the place it belonged to the Jemshidis, subjects of the Ameer. The Sariks formerly dwelt at Merv. In 1856 the Tekkes migrated thither, and afte a struggle compelled the Sariks to withdraw higher up the Murghab. Part of them, as I have said, stopped at Youletan, geo-

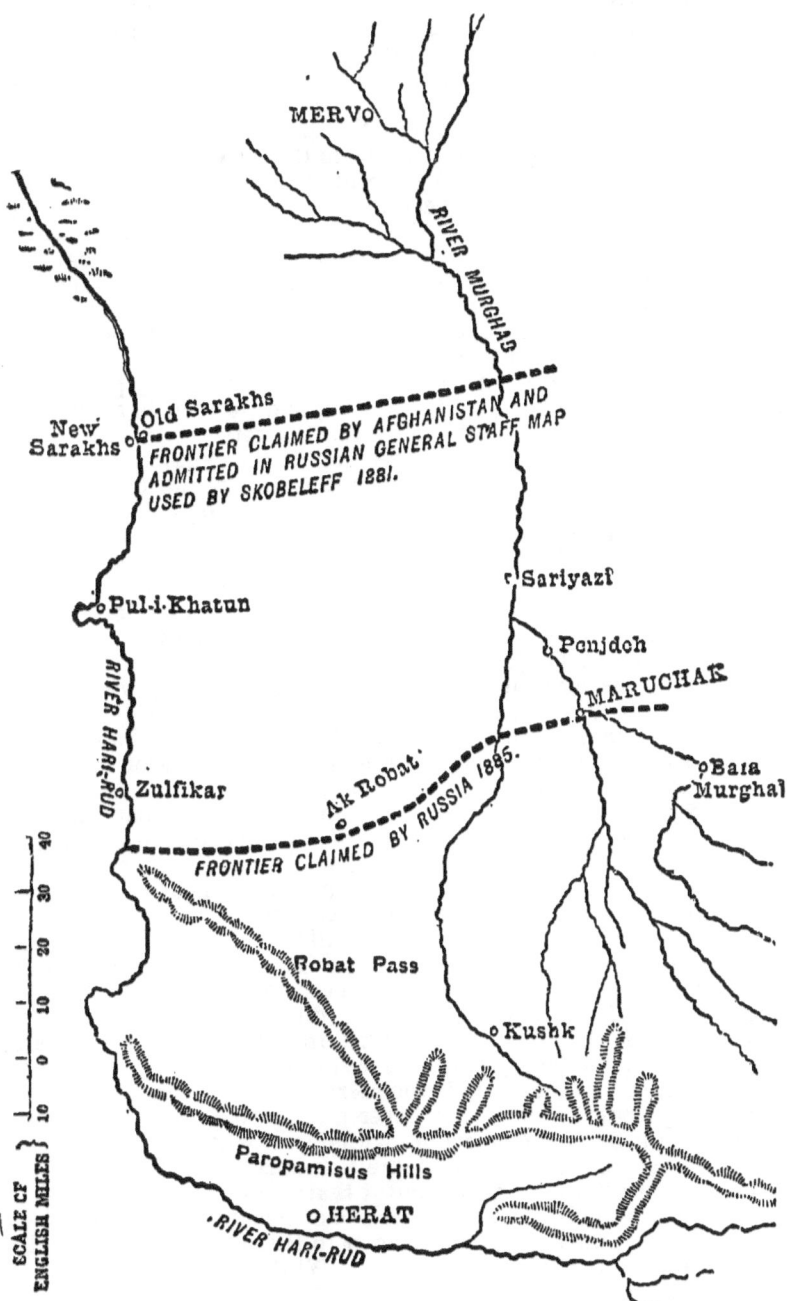

MAP SHOWING THE DISPUTED TERRITORIES.

graphically part of the Merv oasis; but the rest, numbering over 6,000 families, moved higher up, traversing the desert section of the Murghab, and drove the Jemshidis out of Penjdeh. The Jemshidis, in their turn, also moved higher up, to within a short distance of Herat.

But it is well to bear in mind that these Sariks, having seized Afghan lands, paid annually tribute to the Ameer for them. The receipts of the tribute received are contained in the books of the administrative of Herat, and there can be therefore no doubt on this point. It has been said that the tribute was not paid without the dispatch of troops to the district, but this does not invalidate the Ameer's claim. For instance, as I pen this very passage, the tax-gatherer has sent in to say that if my taxes are not paid within three days he will distrain for them. I reply, telling him to be hanged, but this retort to his threat of force does not dispose of the right of the Government to treat me as a subject, and seize my property if the taxes are not paid. In Afghanistan, and, in fact, in all Eastern countries, the soldier is invariably the tax-gatherer. Throughout the whole of the Russian Asiatic dominions the Cossack goes round with the tax-gatherer, and, but for the Cossack, the taxes would very often not be paid. The collection of taxes or tribute at Penjdeh by the occasional dispatch of Herati horsemen, therefore, was simply part and parcel of a prevailing system in the East, and not an exceptional case. The contention that Penjdeh was not an Afghan district because the Sariks (like myself) were sometimes remiss in paying their taxes, will not hold water one moment.

Having treated Penjdeh as an administrative part of Herat so many years, the Afghan authorities were consequently within their rights when they sent a small force there in June or July, 1884, to protect it from seizure by Alikhanoff. They knew how treacherously Russia had acted at Merv, and had every reason to believe that Alikhanoff was bent upon seizing Penjdeh.

I have already said that the subsequent advance twenty miles to Sariyazi was simply the pushing out of a picket to give warning of the expected Russian approach, and that had not Russia seized Pul-i-Khatun, no such movement would have been made. There was, therefore, no provocation on the Afghan side.

With regard to Russia the case was different. Pul-i-Khatun, and the rest of the uninhabited points up the Hari Rud south of Sarakhs, had never been part of the Merv territory, nor had the Mervis ever had control of the districts. Those districts were unprotected, simply because the raids of the Tekkes upon Persia had driven back the people to the Paropamisus or elsewhere, or had exterminated them outright. But although the Mervis raided across the country in pushing toward Persia, they never attempted to hold it; for geographically it had no connection with Merv whatever. The argument has been put forward that the Russians had a right to seize it because it was "unoccupied," but if that argument were allowed to pass, a large proportion of the coast line of Australia could be seized on the same grounds; and, applying it to Russia, hundreds of miles of coast line in the Pacific and on the White Sea would be open to seizure, not being occupied or administered.

If the Afghans had been making preparations to march to Pul-i-

Khatun, there might have been some justification for Komaroff's occupation of it; but they were quietly posted at Penjdeh, awaiting Lumsden's arrival. Before even Lumsden himself could make any preparations of the kind, and give provocation thereby, the Russians had advanced and seized all the territory they could lay their hands on without actually dispossessing the Afghans. In some places they pushed behind the Afghans, as at Ak Robat, which is considerably to the rear of Penjdeh, and within eight miles of Herat.

On this account, I hold that this rush to the gates of Herat was a violent and treacherous proceeding, having all the characteristics of the swoop upon Merv.

While the movement was being made toward Herat, "by the express orders of Prince Dondukoff-Korsakoff," as Komaroff gave out, the Russian Government was effecting an operation of another kind, which indicates the kind of enemy we have to deal with. Imagining there were no experts in London, Lumsden having taken with him Stewart, Napier, and Condie Stephen to the frontier, it suddenly dispatched their own chief agent, Lessar, to this country. Russia delights in strokes of this sort. She always does "the unexpected." In 1878, when we were increasing our fleet to fight her, she suddenly dispatched sailors to America and bought ships, with the intention of slipping out of the Atlantic ports and preying on our commerce. Our fleet she did not mean to notice at all. No country is more ready to discover the weak points of a rival, and to take advantage of them, than Russia. She displayed this clearly enough when she sent Lessar to London.

I say this without making any reflection upon Lessar personally, for my high opinion of him has been repeatedly avowed in my books. I may even go so far as to claim that the reputation which he possessed in the eyes of the public and Government of this country, on his arrival in February, was largely a reputation of my own creation. When Lessar's name was first heard in this country in 1882, it was coupled with the epithet of "spy" and "secret agent." I defended him against those charges. Year after year, as I described his successive explorations in my books,* and expounded their importance, I insisted upon the honest, sincere, and unaffected character of the clever young explorer. This opinion was not simply based upon what had been said to me by his superiors in Russia, but upon what I had heard from Russian friends of mine, who knew him well. I may add that this attitude was not lost upon Lessar, for, shortly after his arrival in London, he thanked me warmly in a letter for the kindly manner I had always referred to his surveys.

Hence, I wish it to be clearly understood that in saying what follows, I am inspired by no animus against Lessar, nor do I wish to excite any prejudice against his person. I criticise his mission, and the Government that created it; if my remarks appear to touch Lessar himself sometimes, I must ask that they be understood as applying to him, not as the eminent explorer, but as the mouthpiece of the Russian Foreign Office.

Up to the time of the swoop upon Merv, Gospodin Lessar was

* "The Russian Advance," 1882; the "Russians at Merv and Herat," 1883; "Reconnoitring Central Asia," 1884.

simply a railway engineer. It was in that capacity he had been dispatched on his first survey in the direction of India in 1881, and he was still a *Tchinovnik* attached to the Ministry of Railways. The Russian Government was perfectly aware of the high estimation in which this railway engineer was held in England. It therefore suddenly turned him into a diplomatist, and, after a decent interval, with equal suddenness sent him to London.

His proper place, of course, was on the Afghan frontier, as adviser to Zelenoï. Russia had no intention of sending Zelenoï thither. She had certainly appointed him before Lumsden left London, but she had only done this to gain time to mature her military preparations for seizing the gates of Herat. Once those gates were seized, she no longer needed a delimitation commission. What she needed was to break down English opposition to that seizure. For this purpose, it was necessary to create a "cave" in English opinion: to divide the country on the subject, and to force the Government to yield to the pressure of accomplished facts.

To realize this treacherous aim Lessar was sent to London.

Without dipping too deeply into a very unpleasant subject, I may recall to the reader the very strong pro-Russian influence that was exercised in 1877-78, through books, pamphlets, and the press, by Madame de Novikoff, otherwise O. K., and the group of admirers she gathered around her. I will not discuss whether that influence was good or bad, but I will point out that it was a strong influence, and that it exercised an effect upon English public opinion and upon the policy of the Government. At any rate, that, at least, was the impression in Russia.

What, therefore, M. de Giers had in view when he dispatched this amiable young traveler, Lessar, to London was, the formation of another pro-Russian party. He trusted to winning the battle of the boundaries, not on the frontier, but in the midst of distracted England.

It was rather cruel, using such a weapon against Mr. Gladstone.

Fortunately, party feeling did not run so high as in 1878, and Lessar found when he arrived a solid block of public opinion opposed to his pretensions. Still, he was not altogether without success. The *Pall Mall Gazette* opened its columns to his pen and became his mouthpiece. The wires of the press were pulled, and all manner of charges raked up against the Afghans. Even Sir Peter Lumsden's mission was assailed.

Let me give an example of some of these unscrupulous charges. On February 24th the *Pall Mall Gazette* published a long letter from Madame de Novikoff at St. Petersburg, in which that lady said that "one who is of the highest authority on all matters relating to the foreign policy of our Empire" had told her Penjdeh had been occupied by the Afghans at the instigation of Mr. Condie Stephen and other subordinates of Sir Peter Lumsden. "I have just had a most interesting conversation," said Madame de Novikoff, "with one who is of the highest authority on all matters relating to the foreign policy of our empire. . . . I asked him to tell me quite frankly the *verité vraie* about our alleged advance in Herat. 'The question,' he replied, 'is as simple as possible. We do not want Herat, and we cannot get it. If we seized it, it would bring us into conflict not only with the Afghans but also with Persia (*sic*), not to speak of England.' 'But,' I rejoined, 'have we not already made a forward movement which we thought unnecessary!' 'Yes,' he answered, 'but do you know how this came to pass? Unfortunately, Sir Peter Lumsden has taken with him two or three young fellows like Mr. Stephen, who speak Russian, and who imagine that they can serve their cause, or the cause of England, by inciting the Afghans to occupy positions in advance of their own frontier. *The Afghans, acting under the instigation of these young Englishmen,* occupied a position at Penjdeh, in territory which had never been under Afghan rule. . . . Our military people, hearing and seeing everywhere evidences of English hostility and English intrigues, immediately responded to the Afghan advance by a further advance on their own account, and they went further than was either prudent or useful. Thus a mistake has been made on both sides, but the initiative has been taken by the English or by those among them who pushed the Afghans forward to go where no Afghan had ever been before.'"

Now there is only one English expression that will fitly describe all the foregoing. That expression is a strong one, but it is no stronger than any judge would apply to it at a court of law. The whole statement is a "pack of lies."

If this expression seems severe it should be remembered that Lumsden and his subordinates, honorable English gentlemen, and not intriguers like Alikhanoff, were far away from home when their character was thus grossly assailed, and that they were traduced by an intriguing agency planted in our midst for the purpose of enabling Lessar to secure for Russia what he could have never obtained by fair argument on the frontier.

In the first place, it was announced in all the English and Russian newspapers before Sir Peter Lumsden, with Mr. Stephen, left England, that the Afghans had occupied Penjdeh, so that the assertion that Mr. Stephen instigated them to do it is absurdly mendacious. Mr. Stephen traveled with Sir Peter Lumsden the whole way, and it was long before they reached the frontier that they heard Komaroff had seized Pul-i-Khatun. The two then proceeded straight to Sarakhs to see Komaroff and protest, and they were told that Komaroff had been ordered to advance by the orders of the Russian Government. Thus we see that the Russians advanced long before Sir Peter Lumsden and his rash "young Englishmen" arrived on the scene, and the statement therefore that they egged on the Afghans, and thereby provoked it, is an obvious falsehood. What I say of Lumsden's own party applies equally to the Indian contingent. The Afghans did not advance an inch after the English arrived at Herat, and as the Pul-i-Khatun movement of Russia was made anterior to our arrival, it is therefore false to say that we incited the Afghans to aggression.

It is unpleasant to have to say it, but Madame de Novikoff is given to making charges of this kind. It would be easy to multiply instances of her "special pleading." Let me quote a characteristic instance. In 1881, while Skobeleff was besieging Geok Tepé a certain Captain Butler, out of a desire for notoriety, wrote to the *Globe,* intimating that he had helped the Tekkes to fortify the place. The assertion occasioned a good deal of annoyance to our government, and being altogether unfounded Butler was placed on the retired list. In Russia, what he said was never taken seriously, and not only did the press pooh-pooh his pretensions, but Skobeleff himself laughed at the idea. My conversation with him on the matter was published in "The Russian Advance Toward India," which book contained further the opinions of Grodekoff, etc., completely disposing of Butler's claim. Not long afterward Madame de Novikoff published a work called 'Skobeleff and the Panslavist Cause." In this she embodied the whole of my conversation with Skobeleff, but suppressed the bit about Butler. Then at the end, when she made an onslaught on Rawlinson and the Russophobes, she penned this assertion: "The Atrek frontier was the line along which your Central Asians and ours elected to fight. *An English officer, Butler, fortified Geok Tepé!"*

Yet O. K. knew when she penned this passage that Butler did not fortify Geok Tepé, and that her idol, Skobeleff, who was surely a good judge, had declared he had not. But she wanted to make a case against England, and was ready to write that black was white, and white was black, in order to further her ends.

The *Pall Mall Gazette* proved an efficient organ for the pro-Russian party. Day after day it formulated the charges against the Afghans, and suppressed facts that clashed at all with its views. An illustration may be given of this. On February 27th it published an article, entitled, "Is Penjdeh in Afghanistan?—by a Russian" (ascribed by the *Moscow Gazette* to Lessar), in which an elaborate attempt was made by references to faulty, obsolete English maps, and the works of two or three careless authors, to prove that Penjdeh was not in the Ameer's dominions. I thereupon wrote a short letter stating the facts about the Russian official maps I have mentioned, and which Lessar had ignored, and I inclosed a fac-simile sketch of the frontier on Skobeleff's map. Both of these were suppressed.

But this was only a minor matter. On the 12th of March it published a special article, with a map, in which it claimed that Lessar's demands were moderate, on the ground that I myself had assigned to Afghanistan a frontier line in 1881 further south than the one he proposed.

I have already spoken of Petrusevitch's idea of thrusting a wedge from Merv and Sarakhs to the gates of Herat. That idea, I mentioned, seemed to me so fraught with danger, that I wrote a book on it—"Merv the Queen of the World"—illustrating the serious character of the claim in a series of maps. On those maps I drew the Afghan frontier as Petrusevitch desired it to be, and I said on the first of the series that the frontier was Petrusevitch's. The whole purport of the book, I should add, was to expose and denounce this pretension. Well, the *Pall Mall Gazette*, ignoring the whole book, tore out one of the maps, and declared that "I" had assigned the wedge frontier to Afghanistan, and had supported it!

Now, if the Russian case was so sound why was all this lying needed? As a retort, let me mention something about the *Pall Mall Gazette*. On the 22d of February, 1884, it published an article with a map, in which it denounced the fuss about the annexation of

Merv, implying it would lead to nothing further, and said that "Mr. Charles Marvin and Mr. Ashmead Bartlett were the only two alarmists in the country." In that map the *Pall Mall Gazette* itself traced the Afghan frontier as running from Sarakhs to Imam Bukush, north of all the country now occupied by Russia.

It was by such artifices as the manipulation of my maps that the pro-Russian party in London did their best to break down English opposition to the Russian retention of the gates of Herat. Lessar's mission was not wholly without success. If he did not create a cave, he made a rift in English public opinion. When he first arrived the Gladstone Government angrily demanded that Russia should immediately withdraw from the gates of Herat. England virtually presented an ultimatum. Before he had been a month in London the Government, yielding to the insidious pressure exercised at home, and the determined front made by Russia on the Afghan frontier, withdrew that ultimatum.

---

## CHAPTER V.

### HOW HERAT IS THE KEY OF INDIA.

Misconceptions respecting Herat—What Russian and English generals really mean when they call it the Key of India—The midway camping-ground between the Caspian and India—Russia's intrusion on the camping-ground —Character of the country claimed or occupied by Russia—Impossibility of severing it from Herat—No mountain barrier whatever between Herat and the new Russian outposts—The tribes on the Russo-Afghan frontier—Russia's design on Afghan Turkestan.

" A BODY of European troops established at Herat, and standing with its front to the south-east, would draw upon it the attention of the whole population of India. In that lies the significance of a military occupation of Herat; and it is not without reason that a number of English experts, knowing India well, have expressed their belief that were an enemy to occupy Herat with a powerful force, the English army, without having fired a shot, would consider itself half beaten."

These words were penned by General Soboleff in 1882. He was then chief of the Asiatic branch of the General Staff, and exercised a large control over the Russian military advance in Central Asia. Subsequently he was appointed Minister of War in Bulgaria, where he distinguished himself by his zeal in Russianizing the country, with the idea of hastening the time for a fresh advance upon Constantinople. More recently he has rendered himself notorious by a fierce tirade against England, published in the *Russ* about a month after the time Komaroff and Alikanhoff insulted Sir Peter Lumsden at Sarakhs.

" Herat is a very large city, and does not cede in size to Tashkent. It contains 50,000 people. Among the cities of Central Asia and Khorassan, Herat, by its buildings, occupies a place next to Meshed. The city is surrounded by walls twelve feet high, with a shallow ditch outside. There are no outer defenses of any kind; nothing that would call to mind the fortifications of a European city. In its present condition Herat is not in a position to defend itself against a European army, since at a mile to the north it is commanded by heights, from which it could be bombarded by artillery. It is reckoned to possess immense strategical importance.''

This brief account was written some years ago by General Grode-koff, the officer appointed by Alexander II. to act as chief of Kauf-mann's staff in 1878, when an attack upon India was projected. After peace was concluded at Berlin, he rode home from Tashkent through Herat, and stayed at the place several days. The opinions of Soboleff and Grodekoff, as military officers of high rank and capacity, are surely worth consideration, yet we have certain polit-ical flounderers in our midst who say that, '' After all, they doubt whether Herat is of any real value to India.''

They say this, ignoring what Sir Henry Hamley, Sir Frederick Roberts, Sir Charles MacGregor, Lord Napier of Magdala, and other great English generals have spoken or written respecting the '' immense strategical importance of Herat.'' The public have their choice. On the one hand are the carefully-weighed opinions of a great array of brilliant soldiers, who have fought and bled for the Empire; on the other is the hare-brained chatter of a few political babblers, who have done their utmost to involve that Empire in its present complications. Now is the time for England to make up her mind about Herat. She can safeguard it, or she can let it drift into Russia's possession. One thing, however, she would do well to realize in time—if *she* does not value Herat Russia does; and Russia values it so much that, by hook or by crook, she means to have it.

To a reporter of the Press Association Lessar said, March 15th: '' We have no intentions on Herat, which is altogether out of the sphere of our action.''

The same Lessar wrote to the *Novoe Vremya* in November, 1883, when the Russian troops were already massing on the Tejend and in Khiva for Alikanhoff's dash upon Merv: '' The longer Merv re-mains independent the better for Russia, its occupation would not be difficult, while possession would be extremely unprofitable.''

On February 29th, 1882, M. de Giers said to Sir Edward Thorn-ton, using the very words employed by Lessar: '' Russia has no in-tentions whatever of occupying Merv and Sarakhs.'' Within two years from this period of '' no intentions '' Merv was a Russian possession.

So that it will not do to rely upon Russia's disinterestedness as a safeguard to Herat. The question, therefore, to consider is—Is Herat worth safeguarding, and can we safely allow Russia to re-main in possession of its gates?

The city of Herat has found an eloquent historian in the person of Colonel Malleson, whose '' Herat: the Granary and Garden of the East '' ought to be read by everybody at this juncture. It is one of the oldest cities in the East, and was once one of the richest. To use the words of a Persian geographer, '' the city has been fifty times taken, fifty times destroyed, and fifty times has it risen from its ashes.'' Six hundred and sixty years ago it contained, accord-ing to the records of the period, 12,000 retail shops, 6,000 public baths, caravanserais, and water mills, 350 schools and monastic in-stitutions, and 144,000 occupied houses, and was yearly visited by caravans from all parts of Asia. When Chingiz Khan passed across the East, devastating the region, Herat is said to have suffered by the two stormings it experienced at his hands a loss of a million and a half of men. In subsequent ages its splendor revived, and it was a great and flourishing city down to comparatively modern times.

Summing up in his masterly manner the career of Herat, Colonel Malleson says: "A glance at the record of the past will show that from time immemorial the city was regarded as an outlying bulwark, the possession of which was necessary prior to attempting the conquest of India; the holding of which by India or by quasi-vassal powers dependent on India, would render impossible an invasion of that country. It was so considered by Alexander, by Mahmud and his successors, by Chingiz Khan, by Taimur, by Nadir Shah, by Ahmad Shah, and by Muhammad Shah, the Persian prince who attacked it in 1837. In the cases of all but the last the possession of Herat led to the conquest of India; in the case of the last the successful defense of that city rendered invasion impossible.

"The hasty reader may object—what can the possession of one city signify? A question of this nature touches the real point of the argument. Herat is called the gate of India, because through it, and through it alone, the valleys can be entered which lead to the only vulnerable part of India. Those valleys, running nearly north and south, are protected to the east by inaccessible ranges, to the west by impracticable deserts. No invading army could dare to attempt to traverse the great salt desert, and the desert immediately south of it, the Dasht-i-Naubad, while a British army held Herat. As long as that army should hold Herat, so long would an invasion of India be impossible. In his masterly lecture at the Royal United Institution, in November, 1878, General Hamley laid down the broad principle that if England were to hold the western line of communication with India, that by Herat and Candahar, she need not trouble herself much about the eastern, or the Cabul line. On the same occasion Sir Henry Rawlinson declared, in reply to a question put to him by Lord Elcho, that rather than allow the occupation of Herat by Russia he would venture the whole might of British India. That high authority saw clearly what I have feebly endeavored to demonstrate in these pages—that the possession of Herat by Russia means the possession of that one line by which India can be invaded; that the possession of Herat by England means the annihilation of all the Russian hopes of an invasion of India. Let the reader imagine that Candahar is the frontier British station; that between Herat and Candahar is a long lane, so protected on both sides that the man who may wish to traverse any part of it to Candahar must enter by Herat. Is it not obvious that the power which shall hold Herat will completely dominate the lane? It is this which makes the possession of Herat by England a matter of vital consequence.

"Another fact illustrates the enormous value of Herat. Place an army there, and nothing need be brought to it from Europe. Within the limits of the Herati territory all the great roads leading on India converge. The mines of the Herati district supply lead, iron, and sulphur; the surface of many parts of the country is laden with saltpetre, the willow and the poplar, which make the best charcoal, abound; the fields produce in abundance corn, and wine, and oil. From the population, attracted to its new rulers by good government, splendid soldiers might be obtained.

"Such are the military advantages presented by Herat to the power that shall occupy it. Should that power be an enemy, Herat would be to him an eye to see and an arm to strike—an eye to pry into every native court of Hindustan, to watch the discontents and the broodings of the rulers, the heart-burnings of their subordinates. From watching and noting to fermenting and stirring up there is but one short step. Evey court, every bazaar, in India, would note the presence on the frontier, in a position not only unassailable, but becoming every day more and more capable of assailing, of a first-class power, the secret enemy of England, and professing the most unselfish anxiety to relieve them in their distress. An arm to strike, because a few years of intelligent rule would render the valley of the Hari Rud capable of supporting and equipping an army strong enough even to invade India.

"In a third sense, likewise, the possession of Herat by an enemy would be not less dangerous to England. The roads converging on it, already alluded to, are traversed by caravans to which no other route is available. We may be sure that the city which successfully resisted the rivalry of Meshed, when Meshed was backed by all the influence of the Shahs of Persia, will take a still higher position when supported by the might either of England or of Russia. The European power whose influence shall be paramount in Herat will rule the markets of Central Asia. More even than that. The possession of Herat by Russia means the exclusion of England from the markets of Central Asia."

The city stands on the right bank of the Hari Rud, from which water is brought by several channels. It is built in the form of a rectangle, the north and south faces being about 1,500, and the east and west faces 1,600 yards in length. Inclosing the city is an immense earthwork about 50 feet high, surmounted by a wall ranging from 25 to 30 feet, with a deep moat, which can be easily flooded from the Hari Rud. The citadel is situated in the center of the city, and is also surrounded by a moat. There are five gates, of which one, however, is closed up, and each is flanked by two bastions. The city is bridged at each of the four gates by a wooden drawbridge, which is raised and lowered by mechanical appliances worked from inside the walls. Each face of the four walls is furnished with from 25 to 30 bastions. On the exterior slope of the embankment, supporting the walls, are two lines of shelter trenches, one above the other, carried all around the city, except where the gates are. A correspondent with Lumsden's mission describes the mounted armament as some "twenty guns of varied calibers, besides numberless others lying dismounted on the ramparts." Twenty guns to defend 3½ miles of wall! The garrison consists of 4,000 or 5,000 troops, exclusive of irregulars.

It may be mentioned that the Russians have complete plans of the fortifications, obtained by General Grodekoff in 1878.

The estimates of the population show considerable divergence. The first during the present century was Christie, who visited the place in 1809, and reckoned the population at 100,000. Burnes and Shakspeare called at Herat on their way north. Conolly was there in 1828-30, and gives 65,000 as the figure; while Pottinger, in 1837-8, states the number at about 40,000; and Ferrier, in 1845, estimated it as low as 22,000. Whether any of the numbers, or all of them, were correct, is impossible to say; but since Herat is a rendezvous for the country people when threatened by the enemy, each estimate may be quite correct for the year stated. Later, in 1865, Pollock again gave 100,000; and in 1878 General Grodekoff thought the approximate number was close on 50,000. The latter figure is now generally accepted by geographers. Candahar has also 50,000 or 60,000 inhabitants. These are the only two towns lying between the Russians and India.

To most Englishmen Herat is associated with the brilliant defense of the city which Eldred Pottinger maintained in 1837 against a Persian army of 40,000 men and 60 guns, commanded by Muhamad Shah. A large number of Russian officers participated in the siege, and an entire Russian regiment. Pottinger, a young Bombay military officer, happened to be exploring in the neighborhood when they arrived, and persuading the Aghans to allow him to control the defense, maintained a desperate resistance of ten months, when the Persians retired. It may be noted that the Persians marched from the Caspian *viâ* Askabad and Meshed to Herat, by a road 550 miles long, running parallel with the one *viâ* Krasnovodsk and Askabad. This road was supposed to be the best highway of invasion to India, but Lessar's discovery of the easy section from Sarakhs to Herat proved the one now held by the Russians to be superior. As the Russians are almost certain before many years are past to absorb Khorassan, the second Transcaspian road will also come into their possession.

In 1881, when English people were still incredulous as the practicability of a Russian invasion, I put forward this argument: that Persia, having in 1837 marched 35,000 troops and 50 guns (composed of 18 and 24 pounders) from the Caspian to Herat, and in 1880, Ayoub Khan, 30,000 troops and 30 guns from Herat to Candahar, to which point various English armies had advanced from the Indus with guns, therefore there was absolutely no physical obstacle to the marching of a powerful Russian force with heavy artillery all the way from the Caspian to India. The terrific mountain barrier many English politicians still believe in, I asserted to be sheer moonshine. Since then, this practicable line of invasion has been supplemented by the second that the Russians now hold, and of which I have said it is so flat and easy that one could drive a four-in-hand all the way to the outposts of Quetta. In the event of war, both routes would be used by Russia.

Since 1856, when Persia advanced a second time and took Herat, for which we went to war with her and made her retire, the Shah's power has been rapidly declining in Khorassan. A detachment of 2,000 or 3,000 Russian troops—even less—planted at Astrabad and Shahrood would sever all communication between Teheran and the rotting, misgoverned Transcaspian province of Khorassan, and Russia could utilize its resources to the fullest extent for an attack upon Herat. Considering how imbecile and corrupt the Shah's rule

is notoriously known to be, it has always seemed in my eyes an as-
tounding piece of bad statesmanship that Lord Lytton should have
entertained for one moment in 1879 the idea of severing Herat from
Afghanistan, and confiding it to the care of Nassr-ed-din. One
might as well have set a mouse to guard a piece of cat's-meat from
a tabby.

In its present condition the fortress of Herat is admittedly not
strong, and it would require a considerable amount of exertion on
the part of the officers attached to Lumsden's mission to render it
secure from a Russian attack. This admitted weakness has given
rise to the remark more than once of late that, such being the case,
we could hardly call it the Key of India.

But this contention, which is mainly put forward by men who
have not taken the pains to read the arguments of Malleson and
other authorities, or who, if they have, from lack of memory have
forgotten them, will not bear serious examination one moment. A
score of the ablest generals of the day, in Russia as well as in England, have declared Herat to be the Key of India. Do you think
that they are likely to be wrong, because some mole-eyed man of
peace has made the discovery that the defenses of Herat are a little
bit out of repair? Admit that they are; what then? Are the military
resources of the Russian empire so meager that, after the Tsar had
seized the place, he can not apply a few patches?

But the issue raised is a totally false one. Concentrating their
gaze too much upon the town, men overlook the locality. What is
the Key of India? On this point a deal of misconception prevails,
which I have been doing my utmost to dispel for a long time.*

In England the impression is widespread that such English generals as MacGregor and Hamley, and such Russian commanders as
Skobeleff and Kaufmann, have concurred in regarding Herat as the
Key of India, solely because it is a great-fortress, or because it may
be made to be one. But these generals have always looked at Herat
in a wider sense, as may be, indeed, almost inferred from the remarks I have quoted of Malleson.

Our generals and the generals of Russia value Herat, not solely on
account of the city; but on account of the resources of the district
in which it is situated—resources in corn and beef, which, if swept
into any point of the Herat district, not necessarily to Herat itself,
would feed an army of at least 100,000 men, and sustain them during
the final advance upon India. It is this great camping-ground,
and not exclusively the town of Herat, that is the Key of India. If
a line be drawn south of Herat 100 miles to Furrah, a second west
70 miles to Kusan on the Persian frontier, and a third 120 miles
north, behind the points occupied by the Russians, a rough idea may
be formed of a district as fertile as England throughout, and possessing marvelous mineral resources. This is the camping-ground,

---

* Let me quote two instances. A correspondent of the *Times of India*, accompanying Ridgeway's force, wrote, in November, that the sight of the Herat
fortifications disappointed him; now he had seen the place, he doubted whether
it was really the Key of India. On the 6th of March, Sir George Campbell,
speaking at a lecture I gave at the Royal Aquarium, also questioned its being
the Key of India, because "the place is very weak, and could be easily taken by
a European enemy."

this is the place of arms, which Russia wants, in order that she may be always able to threaten India. There is no such camping-ground anywhere between the Caspian and Herat, and none again between Herat and India. Hence, not without reason, have the ablest generals of England and Russia designated the district the Key of India.

General MacGregor put this plainly enough in his "Khorassan," in 1875: "From the fort attached to the village I had a fine view of the valley of Herat, which stretched in every direction but the south, one sea of yellow fields and verdant trees. Without going further, it was easy to see the value of Herat to any power with intentions on India, and to recognize the justice of the dictum which termed it the gate of India. Just as in the minor operations of the capture of a city the wise commander will give his troops a breathe, on their gaining the outer defenses, so must every general coming from the west rest his men awhile in this valley. And no better place could be found for this purpose; abundance of beautiful water, quantities of wheat and barley and rice, endless herds of cattle and sheep, good forage, and a fine climate—all combine to make the Herat valley the most apt place for a halt before entering the desolate country between Furrah and Candahar."*

The significance of the recent Russian advance consists in this— that the Russians have established themselves inside the very limits of the Herat district; in other words, they have violated the integrity of the Key of India. Ak Robat, Pul-i-Khisti, etc., which Russia has seized, are inseparable parts of the Key of India. Penjdeh, which they claim, is absolutely essential to its security. These places are included within the fertile zone of Herat. The Russians have crossed the desert zone and established themselves upon it. They have settled down on the edge of the great camping-ground I have described. Shall they remain there? That is the point which England has got to settle. If they do remain—if we resign to Russia the gates of Herat—the Alikhanoffs and the Komaroffs will soon possess themselves of the rest of the great camping-ground, and hold the Key of India.

Most unwarrantably, without provocation on the part of English-

---

* MacGregor thus defined, in 1875, why Herat was the Key of India: "Because it is the nearest and best point at which an invader could concentrate and prepare for an invasion of that country—advantages which it gains from its beautiful valley, the fertility of which is unrivaled in Asia; from its strategical position, which gives it the command of all the important roads to India; from the great strength of its fortress, it being, in fact, the strongest place from the Caspian to the Indus; from its admirable climate, and from the prestige it enjoys throughout Asia. The fertility of its valley, and its capability of maintaining large forces, is proved by the fact that it has been besieged oftener than any other city in Asia, and has always afforded supplies for the armies of both besiegers and besieged. And, it must be remembered, the first have sometimes reached as many as 80,000 men, and have seldom fallen below 30,000; while both have always been composed of undisciplined men, who destroyed nearly as much as they consumed. Besides all the positive and patent advantages which the place itself possesses, Russia in Herat would have an unassailable position from which to threaten us in India, so as to compel us to keep large forces always ready to meet the menace, while she would be able to cast abroad throughout India that 'seething, festering mass of disaffection,' the seeds of a rebellion that would still further cripple us: she would altogether alienate from us the whole of the Afghans and the Persian Khorassanese, and would practically control for her own purposes nearly all their military resources."

3

men or Afghans, Russia has intruded on the fertile zone of Herat. England is within her right in demanding that she shall clear off.

To excuse her seizure, she asserts the necessity for a scientific frontier, and contends that the one she proposes is in every respect as good for the Afghans as for herself. Let us see if that be the case.

Round about Sarakhs, on the Hari Rud, is a certain margin of very cultivable ground, broken by a stretch of less fertile or sterile ground, higher up the river toward Zulfikar. Up the Murghab another, but more thoroughly desert district, separates the Merv zone from Penjdeh. The Sarakhs zone and the Merv zone thus formed two excellent links in the chain of a fortified frontier, running from Askabad to Khoja Saleh, on the Oxus; and the line being that recognized by Russian diplomacy, ought to have been insisted upon as the frontier by the English Government.

As I understand, this was formerly done, but in order not to restrict Russia to an arbitrary line, certain modifications were admitted to be possible. The very utmost limit of those concessions was Pul-i-Khatun, in the Hari Rud, and Sariyazi, on the Murghab. This would have effectually secured Russia all the country belonging to the Sarakhs and Merv districts, with perhaps a trifle beyond; but the security of Herat would not have been so grossly assailed as it is now.

This concession would not have altogether pleased England, for Pul-i-Khatun is a very important strategical point. It is only 80 miles from Meshed, and controls the roads leading thither from Central Asia. Established there, Russia secured a lodgment, so to say, in the Meshed district; and as her designs on that rich city are well known, such proximity was not desirable. It further meant bringing the Cossack 39 miles nearer the Key of India. Still, as I have said, for the sake of an amicable settlement, the country might have tolerated this concession.

But Russia was not content with this. She stepped across this Pul-i-Khatun-Sariyazi line, and traversing the country beyond seized a new line of her own, beginning at Zulfikar and running through Ak Robat to Pul-i-Khisti. This new line was on purely Herati ground, and concentrating what I have to say upon it, I will show what this advanced position is, and how essential it is that Russia should be compelled to fall back to the line which the English Government was, as I imagine, prepared to cede to it.

On the map Herat is shown to have lying north of it a mountain range, called the Paropamisus Mountains, which shields the Herat valley, and is claimed by Russia to be an effectual barrier to the city. Russia knows that the English public is slow in ridding itself of geographical errors, and she therefore talks plausibly of a "mountain barrier, with the passes in Afghan hands," as an admirable frontier for Herat. But this is a trifle. She audaciously puts forward as the spokesman of this pretension the very man who, three years ago, upset geography and the policy of Russia and England in Central Asia, by demonstrating that the Paropamisus was no barrier at all! That man was Lessar.

It is well known to politicians what a shock he administered to

England in 1882, when he pushed on to Herat and found the Paropamisus, hitherto considered to be a mountain block, 15,000 or 20,000 feet high, to be but hills 900 feet or so above the surrounding locality.   Can one call a series of hills, three times the height of St. Paul's Cathedral, "a mountain barrier?"   One might as well call Shooter's Hill Mont Blanc.

Let me quote an extract from the *Times* correspondent accompanying Sir Peter Lumsden, published March 12th.   He says: " You will see on the map that two branches of the Paropamisus run from Herat across Badgheis to the Hari Rud—one north-west (the Barkhut Hills), and the other west.   In reality, only the former exists—the southern branch of the Paropamisus is a shadow, unless, indeed, it is represented by the gentle undulations of gravelly soil, covered with camel thorn and assafoetida, which intervene between Herat valley and the latter.   Thus melts away one of those stupendous natural obstacles to the invasion of Herat, among which optimist imaginations have hitherto gambolled so gayly."

Let us have this clear.   Between the Russian position, stretching from Zulfikar to Pul-i-Khisti, north of the Paropamisus, and the Herat valley south of it, there is only one " range."   That range is full of passes, and on one of them (the Sar-i Chashma) the correspondent stood, and he tells us what he saw, gazing in the direction of the Russian position.   " A striking panorama unfolded itself before us.   A vast sea of grassy billowy downs swept to the foot of the Djam mountains in the far west, and to the north rolled away as far as the eye could see, its undulating surface being only broken by the island hills which inclose the island of Penjdeh.   This, then, was the bleak, sterile, mountainous country which we had thought of with a shiver, when our eyes, tired of staring, glaring deserts, were enjoying the rich fertility of the Herat valley.   Mountainous—as mountainous as the Brighton Downs!   Bleak—the climate of the Engadine in August!   Sterile—groves of pistachio and mulberry trees, wild rose trees, real English blackberry bushes, wild carrots, testified to the richness of the soil, irrigated in many places by mountain streams of the purest water, alive with fish!   And this was autumn, the eve of winter; what then must Badgheis be in spring?   Why it should be named Badgheis (" windy ") I know not, for since we have crossed the Sich Bubak we have been sheltered in its kindly bosom from the fierce biting blasts which never ceased to assail us from Seistan to Kusan.   How it has obtained its reputation for sterility is not difficult to say.   Scarcely an acre of this rich soil is cultivated; scarcely, I say, for a few acres to the north of the Chashma Sabz Pass are rudely tilled by a Turcoman, who acquainted us with his existence by rushing into our camp and throwing himself on the ground with loud cries.   It transpired that he was a servant of one Aziz Sirdar, an ex-Tekke chief of Merv, with whom he had fled from Merv when the Russian occupation was imminent.   He had left his wife and children behind him, and was anxious that when we turned the Russians out of Merv we should restore them to him.   As for Aziz Sirdar, he befriended the Ameer when he fled from Afghanistan and passed through Merv on his way to Khiva.   When trouble befell Aziz Sirdar, and he had to leave Merv, he appealed to the gratitude of Abdurrahman Khan, who had become

Ameer of Afghanistan, and not in vain, for he was presented with a village in the Herat valley and with some land in Badgheis.''

To speak, therefore, of a mountain barrier protecting Herat from the Russian outposts is nonsense. It is a series of downs, traversed by numerous roads, which are only of any difficulty in one or two instances in the section immediately north of Herat. But there is no reason why Russia should take these one or two difficult roads, when there are, as Lessar admits, a score of better ones further west, where an advance can be made more easily. It would be impossible for the Afghans to protect the whole length of the Paropamisus, and the closer, therefore, the Russians get to the downs the more quickly they will be able to step across them into the Herat valley. If they retain what they have, and secure what they claim, the Herat valley will be practically at their mercy.

The fertile country immediately north of the Paropamisus is known as Badgheis, and has always been treated as part and parcel of the district of Herat. It was once a populous, well-cultivated country, and now that the raids of the Merv Tekkes have ceased, tribesmen are flowing to it from all parts of Western Afghanistan. It has no natural connection with the Merv district, nor yet again with that of Sarakhs. On the other hand, there is an inseparable connection between Badgheis and the valley of Herat.

Standing on the summit of the Paropamisus, as the *Times* correspondent recently did, the observer would naturally divide Badgheis into two sections. Gazing down the slopes, he would have on the right hand the Kushk-Murghab region, the objective of the Russian advance from Merv, and the Hari Rud region, the objective of that from Sarakhs. The latter Russia claims because the Salors pasture their flocks there; the former she demands with the Sariks. This is what she calls her " ethnographical claim." She has annexed a number of the Turcoman tribes (in the case of Merv fraudulently), *therefore* she has a right to the rest. If they are not annexed, she says that the frontier will be in a state of constant tumult.

Now, let us see what these turbulent tribes really are. First, let us take the Salors, on whose behalf the Russians demand the Hari Rud section of Badgheis.

Once a great tribe, the Salors were shattered by the Persians in 1838 in punishment for their raids. After this they migrated for a time to Murghab from Sarakhs, where they had been long established, and then settled at Zurabad, a district in Persia, on the west side of the Hari Rud, not far from Zulfikar. After a while they got tired of Zurabad, and returned to Sarakhs. Here the Tekkes fell upon them, seized their cattle and property, and carried the tribe off to Merv. This was in 1871. The tribe then numbered about 3,000 families.

These are facts taken from Petrusevitch's report, which is given in full in my " Merv." While O'Donovan was at Merv, in 1881, the Salors, with the consent of the Tekkes, took their departure. Their proper home was Old Sarakhs, but the Persians would not let them settle there, and made them pass on to Zurabad.

In 1882 Lessar paid them a visit and published a report, which is also given in full in my " Russians at Merv." He confirmed Petrusevitch's statements, and added that they were miserably poor.

Altogether the whole Salor tribe did not number more than 4,000 families, of whom 2,000 only were at Zurabad; 1,000 were encamped with the Sariks on the Murghab (a number of whom appear to have subsequently migrated to Zurabad), 400 were on Russian soil at Tchardjui, 200 on Afghan soil at Maimene, and 100 at Pul-i-Salar, close to Herat.

On the 17th of December, 1884, Lessar delivered a lecture at St. Petersburg on Merv, which I have before me now, and in this he added to the foregoing: " The Salors are extremely poor; they have scarcely any tents; they live in reed huts; cattle they have scarcely any, and their principal occupation is agriculture."

Now we can smash into the lies that have gathered about the Russian claim. First let us put that claim in precise language. Russia demands the whole of the Hari Rud, or western half of Badgheis, including Pul-i-Khatun, Zulfikar, Nihalshini, and practically the whole country south of Sarakhs, to the Paropamisus, and east to Ak Robat, *because*, (1) the Salor tribe has from time immemorial pastured their herds there; (2) because the people can not do without that pasture land; (3) and because the tribe is so turbulent that if it were not annexed there would be no peace on the frontier.

In reply, England, basing her rejoinder on Russian facts, can say this: That the Salors belong to Old Sarakhs, and as that is their favorite district and home and there is plenty of land there, thither they ought to return. That the fact of their having from time immemorial pastured their flocks in Badgheis is untrue; for it is only since 1881 that they have been dwelling at Zurabad, excluding a very brief interval twenty years ago. That they have hardly any cattle now, and therefore do not need the pasture lands. That they are so poor and shattered that they have not perpetrated a raid, or been guilty of turbulence, for nearly a quarter of a century. Finally, that they are not camped (at Zurabad) on Afghan soil at all, but on Persian, and can not be held to have the slightest claim to the unoccupied Badgheis district east of the Hari Rud.

I might add that, so far as is known, the 2,000 or 3,000 miserable Salor peasants at Zurabad have displayed no desire to become Russian subjects. But even supposing they have acquiesced, are we to surrender the whole of the west Badgheis district to Russia on that account, with Zulfikar and other gates of Herat? I say no; and if you, reader, say no with equal firmness, the Russians shall never retain them.

Parenthetically, but none the less seriously, let me point out a great and growing danger arising out of this claim to the Salor Turcomans. If Russia retains the west Badgheis district she will also annex, obviously, Zurabad, on the Persian side of the Hari Rud, and we have no knowledge as to how far that annexation may stretch. In all probability it will extend up to within a short distance of Meshed, because Petrusevitch, who first gave the hint to Russia to push the wedge from Sarakhs and Merv to Herat, urged also that the Persian frontier should be bulged in from the Hari Rud to the capital of Khorassan.[*]

Therefore, let it be clearly understood that if we yield Zulfikar

* This is shown in several maps in my " Merv."

and the western gates of Herat, we not only give Russia control over avenues within one hundred miles of the Key of India, but we also seal the fate of Meshed and the great Persian dependency of Khorassan—the golden country, the granary of Transcaspia.

On that account, when England is asked to surrender a "few miles of barren country" and a "mere bit of pasture land" on "ethnographical grounds," it is well she should clearly realize what she is really asked to do.

No diplomatists, as she should surely know by this time, surpass those of Russia in the art of wrapping up mendacious claims in cotton wool.

Having disposed of the Hari Rud section of the Badgheis district, let us deal with the Murghab. The principal feeder of this river is the Kushk, which rises in the Paropamisus immediately north of Herat, within forty miles, and, flowing parallel with the Hari Rud, joins the Murghab where Fort Ak Tepé controls the Penjdeh district.

The eastern section of Badgheis is claimed with the Sarik tribe and because of that tribe.

Now, I have already shown that the Penjdeh Sariks have never had any wish to be Russian subjects, that they hate the people of Merv, that they are naturally separated from them by a band of desert intersecting the Murghab, which the Russians have crossed; that they have long been subjects of the Ameer, and that the lands they hold are Afghan lands. The Russians, therefore, have not the shadow of a claim to this section. The Sariks of Penjdeh number eight thousand families, and, although they were once great raiders —they were always fighting with the Merv Tekkes—they have become so tame since the Russians occupied Merv and the Afghans Ak Tepé, that the frontier is totally free from turbulence and crime. A correspondent writes from there that scarcely any carry arms; that they are a happy, contented, hard-working people, and that English officers are able to ride about the country provided with no weapons for self-defense.

Russian writers have stated over and over again since 1881 that directly Russia suppressed the raids carried on by the Tekkes of Akhal, the people subsided into hard-working peasants. The same has been the case with the Sariks at Penjdeh. The contention, therefore, that Russia must annex the Sariks, to keep them quiet, is preposterous. What is really wanted is some one to annex the Russians, to keep *them* quiet. They are the "turbulent tribes" on the Afghan frontier.

The special correspondent of the *Daily News* writes from Penjdeh, December 7, that he arrived there, expecting to find the Sariks savage monsters. "There they were before us working in their fields, peaceable, good-natured, and smiling fellows. We had seen them at work some days back, and found them a simple, harmless people. The chiefs of the Sariks have manifested the most friendly feelings toward us. They all express themselves as being most friendly, not only to the Ameer, but also to the British Government."

Now, since the eight thousand Sarik families at Penjdeh are quite content with Afghan rule, and are altogether averse to Russia, why should this country hand them over to the Czar, on "ethnographical grounds," for the sake of a frontier which Russian officials candidly admit among themselves is only temporary? If our *prestige* had not fallen so low, such a monstrous demand would have never been made. Russia has not the slightest right to Penjdeh, and if Englishmen put themselves shoulder to shoulder at this crisis she shall never have it. But there is one thing which must not be lost sight of. In withholding Penjdeh from Russia, we must insist on the evacuation of Ak Robat and Pul-i-Khisti, the retention of which by Russia would render Penjdeh practically worthless.

It is between the Hari Rud and Kushk rivers that the salt lakes lie, which Russia claims with the Sarik Turcomans. If she has no right to the one she has none to the other. It is said that the tribes—men ruled by Russia can not do without these lakes, but this is a wide and hazy pretension. There is any amount of salt in the Caspian region, and eastward of it toward Merv, thus securing Russia's Transcaspian subjects, while, as the Sariks of Penjdeh have been the principal users of those lakes, "the indispensable necessity" of Russia controlling them does not appear very apparent. The amount of salt used by the frontier tribesmen is extremely insignificant, and the fact that Russia should include the claim at all among her pretensions indicates how weak her case is.

Before dismissing Russia's demand for Penjdeh, a few particulars about the locality may not be out of place.

Ak Tepé is the controlling point of the Penjdeh district, and it was there that the Afghans built a fort when they occupied the Sarik locality last year. It is situated on a huge mound (hence its name "White Hill") on a piece of flat alluvial ground, round which the Murghab passes in a winding course before joining the Kushk. The site is on the east, not on the west side of the Kushk River, as represented in some maps; hence, it will be seen, the fort not only controls the junction of the Kushk and the Murghab, but the whole country inside the two rivers up to the hills overlooking Herat. Fort Ak Tepé, with its seventeen guns, is thus in every sense a gate to Herat. That gate the Russians would have seized if the Afghans had not forestalled them. It is included within the territory demanded by Russia. The *Pall Mall Gazette* of March 5 thus described Fort Ak Tepé: "The squabble about this trumpery little Afghan sentry-box placed in the middle of the Sariks, the *majority* of whom are under Russian authority, is simply grotesque." This is the pro-Russian way of putting the case. There are 4,000 Sariks under Russia, and 8,000 under the Ameer. The figures I take from Lessar's lecture delivered last year.

The Penjdeh settlements lie south of the fort, toward Herat, thickly disposed round the village of Penjdeh six miles from Ak Tepé, and afterward stretching forty miles or so higher up the Murghab to within sight of the Afghan stronghold of Bala Murghab.

When Russian statesmen speak of Penjdeh they do not mean simply the village of that name, but the whole Sarik district, with Fort Ak Tepé. As that fort is the principal military point of the district, it would have saved some mistakes (?) if more prominence had been given to Ak Tepé and less to Penjdeh. Let me cite one of these "mistakes." To excuse the Russian advance, a certain Radical paper declared that the Afghans had advanced thrice toward Merv—first from Herat to Penjdeh, second from Penjdeh to Ak Tepé, and third from Ak Tepé to Sariyazi! As a matter of fact, the Afghans have only made one advance. They planted themselves at Ak Tepé last year, and it was only to "feel" a rumored Russian advance, after the seizure of Pul-i-Khatun, that they threw ahead the temporary Sariyazi picket that successfully heralded Alikhanoff's raid, and saved Ak Tepé from a surprise.

Subsequently, however, the Russians seized Pul-i-Khisti, or the Brick Bridge, a bridge of nine arches spanning the Kushk a few miles from Fort Ak Tepé; and leading to the entire Penjdeh district. Its retention would render the Afghan fort almost untenable. But this is not the worst. They claim Chaman-i-Bed, between thirty and forty miles up the Kushk, and have already seized Ak Robat, a place possessing an amazing supply of water between it and the Hari Rud at Zulfikar. If they be allowed to remain at Ak Robat they might just as well have Penjdeh, for they will be able to sever it from Herat at any moment. At Ak Robat they are within eighty miles of Herat. Penjdeh is variously stated to be from 100 to 140 miles from the Key of India. The Russians, thus, are a long way to the rear of the Afghans.

Penjdeh is not a simple oasis, like Merv, that can be dissevered from Herat. The Sarik settlements stretch up to those of the Jemshidis, and the Jemshidis, again practically up to Herat. One might as well assert that the French located at Canterbury would not endanger London, as that the Russians at Penjdeh would not be a menace to Herat.

The Jemshidis are very different from what they were when Vambery trudged through their country to Herat. Even Grodekoff in 1878 spoke highly of them. Writing from the spot, the *Times* correspondent attached to Lumsden's force says of them: "They resemble the Turcomans in dress and manners, but they are apparently a quiet, peaceable people. An English officer might safely live among them without any guard, and if they have only respite from raids and war they will doubtless spread over and multiply in the more healthy but deserted lands of Badgheis. They are hardy, clever horsemen, and every household breeds its own horses. When we were in Kushk the weekly fair was held: it was attended by many Turcomans from Penjdeh and by some Firuzkuhis, but by very few Hazaras, with whom the Jemshidis are not on very friendly terms. The Turcomans brought salt, rice, soap, carpets, horses, sheep, and found for sale in the bazaar plowshares (of cast iron) and hatchets from Maimene; Russian and French loaf sugar, Austrian matches, also Bryant and May's, Meshed and Bokhara silk and cotton goods. The greater part of the latter was Russian, not English—let Manchester draw its own conclusion."

Kushk is the central point or capital of the Jemshidis, and it is situated on the Paropamisus, close to Herat. There are about 4,000 families in the place. Telegraphing from it some time ago the correspondent of the *Times of India* said: "The climate and temperature are delightful. The soil is capable of immense fertility, and could support a large population." Even forty years ago, Abbolt, who traversed the Kushk valley, described it to be "highly susceptible of culture, and has been once well tilled."

If the Russians secure Penjdeh, they will have practically no obstruction up to Herat, except the Kushk Pass, which might be avoided in time of war, while in time of peace the intercourse existing between Penjdeh and the adjacent Afghan country would enable them to diffuse their influence far to the south of Herat. This intercourse is not to be lost sight of. The Sariks are not within the commercial orbit of Merv but within that of Herat. It requires little imagination to realize the advantage Russia would gain for intrigue if we allowed her to obtain the district.

On the Murghab itself Russia demands Marutchak, an old Afghan town twenty-eight miles above the settlement of Penjdeh, and eighteen from the Afghan fort of Bala Murghab. Marutchak, on the right or east bank of the Murghab, was anciently a large and prosperous town; "now," says Mr. Simpson, "it is nothing but ruins. The Afghans are at present placing it in a state of repair. The outer wall is only of mud, or sun-dried bricks, and is, in some parts, in a very decayed condition. Over these walls the top of the citadel may be seen. This is one of the old mounds, of which we have observed similar remains in this country. It measures about eighty by seventy yards on the top. The old walls and towers are now being put in a condition of defense. From this citadel there is a great ramp, which runs in a circular form, from the north-east corner to the south-east corner. It is most probably the old wall, inclosing what had been the town at one period; the ramp has much the appearance of being the remains of a mud wall which has crumbled down into dust. The Afghans are now repairing it all round, so as to make it an enceinte for barracks, so that it will accommodate troops. The outer wall, already described, is to be leveled, as being too large for the garrison which the Afghans can afford to keep in it. There are the remains of a few mud houses within the outer wall; but, with the exception of the Afghans employed on the fort, there are no inhabitants."

Bala Murghab is situated on the high road from Afghan Turkestan (Balkh, etc.) to Herat, and thus controls a Russian advance from that direction. The Ameer has recently located 1,000 Jemshidi families there, and is doing his best to make it a great stronghold. If, however, the Russians retain Pul-i-Khisti, and secure Penjdeh, they will be able to sever Bala Murghab from Herat, and the whole of Afghan Turkestan will lie open to them. In securing the eastern gates of Herat, therefore, Russia will obtain a basis for grasping, in turn, the whole of the Ameer's dominions north of the Hindoo Koosh.

The occupation of West Badgheis is a menace to Meshed; the occupation of East Badgheis a menace to Maimene, Balkh, and other outposts of Cabul. The occupation of the two districts jointly is a menace to the security of Herat. Thus the wedge which Russia has driven from Sarakhs and Merv to the gates of Herat opens up a vista of intrigue and annexation to her Komaroffs and Alikhanoffs, which must be to them and to her statesmen positively thrilling.

Hence the quarrel is something more than a mere squabble over an "Afghan sentry box." Without going into the wider issues, and confining ourselves to Herat, we might, to all practical purposes, allow the Russians to occupy the suburbs of Herat as well as let them remain where they are.  All that would be necessary for Russia at any time would be to blockade Herat with a small force, and from her numerous new positions she could sweep up in a few days the whole of the resources that render Herat of value without taking the trouble to fire a shot at the city.  Were the resources of the Key of India contained inside the city of Herat there would be some excuse for leaving the Russians at Ak Robat and other Afghan points, and contenting ourselves with replacing the mud walls with impregnable fortifications; but, since the resources lie spread over the great camping-ground I have described, stretching north and south of the Paropamisus Downs, England can not but resent attempts to fasten a hold upon any part of it.  To violate the integrity of one part of the Key of India is to impair the value of the whole of it.  If we ought to fight for the whole we ought to fight for the part; and, since Russia seems determined to follow up every concession by making still more exacting demands, she really leaves us no other alternative than to resist her claims to the utmost.

England is most decidedly in the right, and Russia most decidedly in the wrong.  It is better that we should fight her now, when she has only got 10,000 troops in the Transcaspian region, and has not thoroughly established herself in the Herat district, than give in now, and have to fight her next year, or the year after, when she has seized the whole of the camping-ground, and concentrated 100,000 troops upon it to drive us out of India.

----

## CHAPTER VI.

### SKOBELEFF'S PLAN FOR THE INVASION OF INDIA.

Skobeleff's great aim in life—The solution of the Eastern Question on the Indian frontier—His plan for invading India in 1876—Adopted before the walls of Constantinople in 1878—Kaufmann's advance toward India—Great changes in Central Asia since—Were Skobeleff alive, his plan would be totally different now—What it would probably be—Feasibility of the invasion of India from the point of view of various Russian generals.

" The probability of our having to struggle for Herat, or to defend India from Candahar, is so remote, that its possibility is hardly worth considering."

These words were penned by Sir Henry Norman, in a memorandum against the retention of Candahar, September 20, 1880.  They illustrate, in a plain and forcible manner, the view of the few, and now utterly discredited experts, who raised their voice in favor of the " scuttle " from Candahar, and invoked the spirit of faction to sanction it.

To-day England is not only morally struggling for Herat, but her Sikhs with Ridgeway at Penjdeh confront the Cossacks with Ali-khanoff at Pul-i-khisti.  At any moment shots may be fired, and then the troops that scuttled from Candahar will have to rush back " to defend India from it."

On the 10th of January, 1881, the Duke of Argyll said, in denouncing Lord Salisbury's avowal of alarm at the advance of Sko--

beleff to Geok Tepé: "We are told by the late Government that the danger they wished to guard against was the danger of a military basis to be formed by Russia on the Caspian. I hold that to be one of the wildest dreams ever entertained."

In four short years the "wildest dream," which, I should point out, was simply the sober military opinion of Valentine Baker, Major Napier, and General Sir Charles MacGregor, who had surveyed the proposed line of advance—in four short years that "wildest dream" has become a practical reality, and the public read, quite as a matter of course, of Russia's preparations for the invasion of India.

Whether the evacuation from Candahar was politic or not in 1881, one thing is certain. Down almost to the very last days of his Viceroyalty, the Marquis of Ripon refused to take serious steps to render the Afghan barrier a real bulwark to our Eastern Empire. The Cabinet in London moved somewhat with the times but, Lord Ripon and Sir Evelyn Baring resisted every change. It is a matter of common notoriety at Simla that the appeals of our greatest generals were pooh-poohed, and that to the very moment of the departure of the Baboo Viceroy from Bombay, the advice of heroes who would have to defend Afghanistan to-morrow, if attacked, was contemptuously rejected for the ear-whisperings of two or three insignificant men, of ignominious sentiments.

Why those generals—who, by the way, are now the chief advisers of Lord Ripon's sagacious successor—should have been so uneasy during the last few years, will be apparent in the following pages.

Until the time of the arrival of the Stolietoff Embassy at Cabul, the idea of a Russian attack upon India was generally scouted in this country; and even those who urged the stemming of the Russian advance did not treat an expedition against us as a matter of the immediate present, but as belonging to the future. In Russia, military opinion was more advanced. While war was still undeclared against Turkey in 1876, and England was hoping that the conflict might be averted by peaceful diplomatic means, General Skobeleff, then Governor of Ferghana, the Turkestan district nearest India, forwarded to Kaufmann an elaborate plan for a Central Asian campaign. Even when summoned to Europe to take part in the operations there, he used his utmost influence at Court to put the Turkestan forces in motion, and finally achieved his object in sight of Constantinople, when, after several councils of war, it was decided that if the Congress at Berlin failed, an attack should be made upon India.

Accordingly, Colonels Stolietoff and Grodekoff left the camp for Central Asia, the former charged with a mission to Shere Ali, and the latter—Skobeleff's oldest and most trusted friend—carrying Skobeleff's secret plans, and for himself the special appointment as chief of Kaufmann's staff. One other agent was also sent from the camp—Pashino, an ex-diplomate, who had served as interpreter at Samarcand to the present Ameer, Abdurrahman Khan, and possessed a knowledge of India from a journey he had undertaken through the peninsula a few years earlier. His mission was to proceed to India and secretly ascertain the condition of military and tribal affairs on the frontier, and afterward push his way through the Khyber and join the Russian mission at Cabul.

The outcome of the enterprise is well known. Kaufmann marched with the invading force to Djam, on the Bokharan frontier, and marched back again when the Treaty of Berlin became known. Stolietoff penetrated to Cabul, and occasioned the Afghan war. Grodekoff returned to Europe by a famous ride through Herat, and is now Acting-Governor of Turkestan. Finally Pashino was arrested at Peshawur, and, in spite of his outcry, was sent back to Russia.

Most of these facts are known to the public, but Skobeleff's proposed plan of operations has never received due attention, even at the hands of those commonly supposed to be interested in Central Asian affairs. Briefly, the plan was this: Kaufmann was to have led an army to Cabul, almost denuding Turkestan of its garrison, and was to have there organized the Afghan forces for an attack upon India, while Russian emissaries stirred up the natives to a mutiny. If the people failed to respond to the Russian appeal, Kaufmann was to tie the English army to India by threatening it from Cabul, and, in the event of a rising, he was to push on to the frontier, and attack the English on one side while the mutineers advanced and harried them on the other. Supposing the attempt failed, Kaufmann was to retreat, not upon Turkestan, in case the sight of his shattered forces should cause Bokhara to rise, but upon Herat and the Caspian; being met on the way by a succoring army advancing *viâ* Askabad and Meshed.

Such was Skobeleff's daring scheme, the revelation of which, since his death, has exercised a remarkable effect upon the imagination of Russian generals, and caused a longing to lead or participate in a campaign offering so many chances of distinction and glory. Had the Congress of Berlin failed, the impression is general among Russian military men that Skobeleff's plan would have been crowned with success. Their belief in the certainty of a mutiny in India is one that Englishmen will not generally share, and hence the probability of an actual irruption into India will be contested; but there is one matter upon which not much difference of opinion can prevail. The Afghans would have doubtless fallen in with the Russian plans, and by their co-operation tied the English troops to the frontier; thereby preventing the re-enforcements being sent to Europe. This alone would have been a success of no mean order, for it is no secret that Russia was greatly disturbed by the idea of Sepoys being dispatched to Turkey to assist in the defense of Constantinople.

Strangely enough Skobeleff's plan of invasion has only excited Russia and England since his death. The actual march by Kaufmann toward India provoked little or no attention in this country, and, the details being suppressed in Russia, it was treated as a simple demonstration intended to give weight to Stolietoff's mission. That it was really a serious move, inspired by the deadliest intentions against our rule in India, was only to the most limited degree realized even by the oldest politicians in this country. The military movement was looked upon as subsidiary to the political mission at Cabul, instead of the latter being, as it really was, a pioneering feeler of the former. This indifference to Kaufmann's march was increased by the English disasters in Afghanistan and Lomakin's failure to conquer the Turcomans. It was asserted that while the Afghan and Turcoman barriers existed India was perfectly safe from attack. Then stress was laid upon the Hindoo Koosh, and politicians overlooked the looming advance from the Caspian. Even Skobeleff's decisive success at Goek Tepé did not shake the belief of the Gladstone Cabinet in the sound and permanent character of the barriers beyond, intervening between Askabad and India. The Duke of Argyll said that the new advance was not to be compared with the older ones, and that we had nothing to fear from Skobeleff's triumph. But for the energy displayed by Lord Salisbury, the fall back from Candahar would have been followed by the evacuation of Quetta.

It was while things were in this condition that Mr. Joseph Cowen, M.P., asked me to proceed to St. Petersburg to ascertain the Russian view of the position in Central Asia from the lips of the principal generals and statesmen. Of all the generals I saw, Soboleff was the only one who would agree with the opinion I strongly held at the time, and which was well known to them, that a Russian attack could be made upon India from the Caspian. General Skobeleff was the most incredulous of all. He would not hear of a Russian attack. "The Central Asian difficulty is all humbug," he said. "I do not think a Russian invasion of India would be feasible. I do not understand military men in England writing in the *Army and Navy Gazette*, which I take in and read, of a Russian invasion of India. I should not like to be commander of such an expedition. The difficulties would be enormous. To subjugate Akhal we had only 5,000 men, and needed 20,000 camels. To get that transport we had to send to Orenburg, to Khiva, to Bokhara, and to Mangishlak for animals. The trouble was enormous. To invade India we should need 150,000 troops—60,000 to enter India with and 90,000 to guard the communications. If 5,000 men needed 20,000 camels, what must 150,000 need! And where could we get the transport? We should require vast supplies, for Afghanistan is a poor country, and could not feed 60,000 men; and we should have to fight the Afghans as well as you. If we bribed one Sirdar, you would bribe another; if we offered one rouble, you would offer two; if we offered two, you would offer five—you could beat us in this. No; the Afghans would fight us as readily as they fought you. I believe the new frontier is quite permanent, and that we shall hear no more about Central Asia for many years to come."

"But in regard to the possibility of invading India, General Soboleff expressed to me a clear conviction that Russia could march an army on India if she chose."

"That was diplomacy," replied Skobeleff. "Of course it is possible—all things are possible to a good general—but I should not like to undertake the task, and I do not think Russia would. Of course, if you enraged Russia—if, by your policy, you excited her—if you made her wild—that is the word—we might attempt it, even in spite of all the difficulties. For my part, I would only make a demonstration against India, but I would fight you at Herat." He said this with great animation, but very good-humoredly. "Do you know, I was very much interested during your war whether you would occupy Herat or not. It would have been a mistake if you had done so. It would be difficult to march an army from the Caspian to Herat to fight you there, but we should be tempted to do it in the event of a war." *

Whether these were really the sentiments of Skobeleff at the moment, or whether he was purposely minimizing the possibility of attacking India, in order that England might not be terrified into preparing against it in time, is a matter over which much argument might be expended without leading to any satisfactory result. I will not attempt to discuss the point. I will simply point out one or two facts, which are of more importance at the present moment.

After Skobeleff had finished his conversation with me he repeated it to Captain Masloff, one of his favorite officers. Masloff published an account of it in the *Novoe Vremya* which tallied with my own, and he subsequently told me that Skobeleff had spoken of my report as perfectly accurate. The part I have repeated in this book was triumphantly quoted by Madame de Novikoff (otherwise O. K.), two years ago as demonstrating the madness of the Russian scare in this country. But O. K. has never said since that these utterances of Skobeleff fell completely flat in Russia. No Russian newspaper, and no Russian military writer has ever reciprocated those views, or, indeed, ever noticed them at all. On the other hand, Skobeleff's opposite opinions in favor of an expedition to India, which began to appear a few months after his death and have been seeing the light at intervals since, have exercised an enormous influence on the Russian military mind. Many of the documents published were written anterior to his conversation with me, but while the latter is ignored and forgotten, the former are incessantly being cited in proof of what Russia can effect against India.

Several other circumstances have contributed to add to the effect of Skobeleff's aggressive views. A few months after his death General Soboleff published his "Anglo-Afghan Conflict," a bulky three-volume work, compiled by the Chief of the Asiatic branch of the General Staff before proceeding to Bulgaria as Minister of War. This work was a sort of official history of our Afghan campaign, based on English sources, and was recommended by the General Staff as a standard work for military libraries. His recent utterances in the *Russ* have shown that General Soboleff looks at things through very peculiar spectacles. He is dominated by the bitterest hatred against England, and believes everything said or written to her disadvantage. In this history he sought to make out, or, it would be better to say, did make out, to his own satisfaction, that the Afghan war was too large an enterprise for us, that we were defeated by the Afghans throughout the campaign instead of being mostly victors, and that we were compelled at last to withdraw owing to the damage inflicted on our prestige and the fear of a rising in India.†

An English reviewer, noticing Soboleff's work, said it was made

* "The Russian advance toward India," page 105.

† A translation of all that is essential in this work is given in "The Russians at Merv and Herat."

up of "lies and nonsense." Upon him, of course, the work made no favorable impression, and he was disposed to minimize its importance. But, as a matter of fact, the book exercised an influence which is displayed pretty clearly to day. To Russian officers who had not studied the subject, or who had only derived their impressions of the war from the jaundiced statements in the Russian press, the book appeared as worthy of credence as any official work could possibly be. It had been compiled by the Chief of the Asiatic branch of the General Staff, whose express duty it was to watch the war on behalf of the Government and obtain all possible information from England—perhaps India—bearing upon it. If such an official did not know what he was writing about, who in Russia was more competent than he? Thus Soboleff's book was eagerly read and widely read, and strengthened to a remarkable degree the feeling already prevailing that we were a very weak military power, and only maintained our hold on India by a miracle.

Skobeleff's opinion that we could be expelled from the peninsula by means of a hard blow struck in front, simultaneously with a fomented mutiny at the rear of the Indus, has excited more and more attention as Russia has approached nearer our outposts. The belief in its feasibility that has steadily developed in Russia, since his plan of 1876 became known in 1885, has received a considerable impulse from the disappearance of the physical obstacles already existing. Skobeleff's main argument against the feasibility of an invasion, when he discussed the subject with me, was the difficulty of transport, but this is a difficulty that has been daily wearing away ever since. When he proceeded to Geok Tepé in 1880 it took nearly a month for the troops of the Caucasus army to march from Tiflis to the Caspian to join. By the opening of the Tiflis-Baku railway, since his death, the journey can now be done between sunrise and sunset. When he ferried those troops across the Caspian he had to contend with a very limited marine. By the development of the Baku petroleum industry fifty powerful steamers, 150 to 250 feet long, have been added during the last few years to the shipping of the Caspian, and can now convey the largest conceivable army across the sea to Krasnovodsk. The Transcaspian railway, again, was not finished to Kizil Arvat until long after he left Geok Tepé. It is now being pushed on to Askabad, and Lessar has stated that whether there be peace or war, it will be continued to Sarakhs—within six marches of the Key of India. Finally, Skobeleff imagined, or said he imagined, a difficult road to exist between Askabad and Herat. Lessar has since discovered that it is one of the easiest in Asia.

Thus, by Russia's resolute destruction of the Turcoman barrier, and by the rapid disappearance of a series of obstacles, things have come to this pass—that a land march upon India to day is an enterprise less difficult to the Russian military mind than the march upon Constantinople in 1877.

Such an enterprise might take two forms. Either Russia might adopt Skobeleff's idea of a fomented mutiny, and advance with merely sufficient troops to cleave a passage through the Afghan barrier, or she might ignore for the moment the people of India, and push on with some such army of mammoth proportions as she employed in the last Russo-Turkish war.

Let me deal with the former first.

At the outset I must point out that a wide difference of opinion exists between English politicians and Russians, as to the possibility of a mutiny in India, and that this deserves more attention than light-hearted publicists in this country are disposed to give it. English politicians generally assume that India is safe, or sufficiently safe, from the danger of another mutiny. Disturbances, it is admitted, might arise on the Russian approach, but the country generally would stand by us. I do not say that all politicians share this optimist view, but the majority do—or at any rate, they conceal their uneasiness and keep it from the public.

Now Russian Generals, and the entire Russian Press, incline to a totally different opinion. General Skobeleff, General Soboleff, General Tchernayeff, General Kaufmann, General Grodekoff, General Annenkoff, General Petrusevitch, and others less known, may be cited as eminent representative Russian military men who never entertained a doubt on the subject. I have discussed the Anglo-Russian conflict with many Russian officers—some of them personal friends of mine—but have never met one who differed from them in this matter. Yet some have made a special study of India. Skobeleff was always purchasing English books on the country, and I question whether there are half a dozen Members of Parliament who have such a good collection of English and foreign books on India as I have pulled about in the library of General Annenkoff.

If we examine more closely the plans of Skobeleff and others, we shall see how important this factor of a general rising really is. Skobeleff put the wants of Russia in a neat, compact form the other day when he declared that "Russia does not want India: she wants the Bosphorus." The Russian invasion of India is commonly ridiculed by certain Radicals on the ground of the hugeness of the enterprise. They assert that the people would never exchange English for Russian masters, and that it would require a larger army than ever Russia could spare to occupy and hold the country. But such assertions are based not upon facts, but illusions. Russia does not propose to occupy and hold India. I have never met a Russian who proposed—at any rate, for the present—such a difficult enterprise as that. Russia does not aim at replacing our administration by her own. None of the Russian generals ever suggested saddling their country with such a burden. What Skobeleff really planned and advocated was, that the 250,000,000 people should be encouraged and helped to throw the 100,000 English off their backs, and that during the universal collapse of our supremacy throughout the world that would ensue (in his opinion), Russia should occupy Constantinople.

Such an enterprise is quite a small affair, compared with the undertaking imagined by those Radicals I have referred to. To secure its success, supposing India to be ready to rise and throw us off. all that is needed is to march to Candahar a force sufficiently strong to overcome the English force holding the frontier; after which the Princes and the mutinous Sepoys themselves could be left to deal with the small garrisons located on the plains and plateaux of India, aided, perhaps, by a few Russian officers. When Skobeleff proposed his plan in 1876, the Russian outposts were too far from the Indian frontier, and the communications connecting them with Russia proper too extended and ill-developed to allow of more than a small force being sent to attack India.   He, therefore, had to rely upon Afghan help on the one hand, and an Indian mutiny on the other.

It is well to notice that he provided for two kinds of assistance in his plan.*   If the Afghan co-operation had been slight, he would have stimulated a general rising in India.   If, on the other hand, he had considered himself sufficiently strong with Afghan help, to break through the frontier, he would only have "manipulated the disaffected elements in India to Russia's advantage."   The possibility of a general rising in India may be questioned by English politicians; but there is not one who can deny that "disaffected elements" do exist in the country.

The genuine belief of Russia in the probability of a mutiny in India on the approach of a small force against us, is too serious a factor in politics to be brusquely treated as an illusion.   The more feasible a Russian attack upon our rule in India appears to the Russian Government, the less disposed will it be to treat us with diplomatic deference in Europe, and refrain from aggressive acts in Asia.   Further, the greater the chances seem to it of a successful campa'gn on the Indian frontier than in Europe, the stronger the impulse to break through the Afghan frontier, at any cost and secure Herat.   What would Russia care for the Ameer's ill will at seizing Herat if she were sure of an Indian mutiny?   The more, therefore, she relies on an Indian revolt the less she may be expected to care for Afghan susceptibilities.

Russia, in a word, has two cards to play—the Afghans and people of India.   If she finds she can not accomplish her aims with the one, she will try to effect them with the other.

"England lays a heavy hand on her dependent peoples," wrote General Soboleff in the _Russ_ last January, when he was already aware that Russia had seized the approaches to Herat.   "She reduces them to a state of slavery; only that English trade may profit and Englishmen grow rich.   The deaths of millions in India from starvation have been caused indirectly by English despotism.   And then the press of England disseminates far and wide the idea of Russia being a country of barbarians.   Thousands of natives in India only await Russia's crusade of deliverance!

"If Englishmen would only throw aside their misplaced pride, and study a little deeper the foundation of Russia's rule in Central Asia, comparing it with their own, they would soon see plainly why the name of Russia has such _prestige_ in Asia, and why the natives of India hate the dominion of England, and set their hopes of freedom upon Russia.   Russia gives full liberty to native manners, and not only does not overburden her subjects with fresh taxes, but even allows them exemptions and privileges of a most extensive character.   England, on the contrary, is a vampire, sucking the last drop of blood out of India.

"As to our course of antagonism in Asia, England herself threw

* I may state that his plans are given in full in "The Region of the Eternal Fire."  London: W. H. Allen & Co., 1884.

down the glove at Sebastopol, and if the Russian flag now floats over Merv, the English have themselves to blame. We accepted their challenge; it now rests with them whether there is to be a Russian invasion of India or not. But we hope the time has come when English strategists will take into consideration the 200,000 troops of the Caucasus, and the 100,000 in reserve of Turkestan and Western Siberia, besides another army of half a million behind in European Russia, and will look on the map and see what must happen if a Russian corps of 200,000 men, accompanied by another of 100,000 of splendid irregular cavalry, pass through Herat and Balah into India, and proclaim the independence of the native population. Let England think well of the consequence of Russia deciding to take up arms against her."

By ignorant or interested writers these threats were represented as merely the casual frantic outpourings of a headstrong and harmless general. But it is well there should be no misconception on this score. Soboleff is an officer of very considerable weight and standing in Russia, and what he said represents fairly the feeling of the whole army and the greater part of the press at the present moment.

All the more reason, therefore, why we should cling to our hold upon Herat, and insist on a settlement of the frontier dispute before Russia masses a force at its gates capable of crushing Lumsden and his Afghan allies.

Let us now consider the second form an attack upon India might take—*i.e.*, a blow delivered by a large army instead of by a relatively small force, and operating without reliance upon a simultaneous rising on the part of the Indian people.

It is no secret that the Government are perfectly aware that Russia could dispatch a very strong expedition to the gates of Herat, and that the calculations as to what she could really do have been scientifically worked out by the ablest English military authorities, in a manner very alarming to those who hold the reins of power in this country. Soboleff's sneering suggestion that English strategists should take into consideration what Russia could accomplish from her Caspian base, in the event of war, has already been anticipated by our generals. They demonstrated, before even Merv was annexed and the gates of Herat were won, that Russia could in 77 days mass 23,000 troops at Herat, and in six weeks afterward at least as many more, while in from 70 to 100 days she could put 13,000 men into Cabul, and in 90 days push 11,000 more into the northern passes of India. Without counting the latter, we may therefore say that before even the last two advances took place in Central Asia, from Askabad to Merv and from Merv to the Paropamisus approaches, our military authorities knew that in less than four months Russia could mass nearly 50,000 men—all Russian troops—on the camping-ground of the Key of India.

A year ago, before these calculations became bruited abroad, I drew attention, in a pamphlet,* to the facility with which Russia, *viâ* the Volga and the Caspian base, could thrust a large army along

---

* " Russia's power of seizing Herat and concentrating a force to threaten India." London: W. H. Allen & Co., 1884.

the Askabad-Herat route to confront us at Candahar, in the event of European complications.   Fresh evidence has accumulated since of the aggressive strength of this line of operations, and it may be that events will practically test it before long.

The Russian army, on a peace footing, numbers between 800,000 and 900,000 men.   In time of war two or three millions may be summoned under the flag.   Every year nearly 300,000 recruits are drafted into the army.

GENERAL SIR F. S. ROBERTS, V.C., K.C.B.

Moscow and the contiguous provinces are generally regarded as constituting the heart of Russia.   If one will take a map, he will see that the distance is no further from this center of strength to Krasnovodsk, on the Caspian, than to Constantinople.   In 1877–8 Russia dispatched nearly half a million men, with an enormous quantity of stores, in the direction of the latter place.   To-day it would be as easy, or rather, easier, to deflect that number upon the Caspian.

Most of the troops sent to the Balkan peninsula, in 1877, proceeded by rail, and it is well known that half of Russia's difficulties arose from the restricted character of his means of communication. But the Volga and its tributaries drain the heart of Russia I have referred to, and constitute a magnificent waterway to the Caspian Sea.

Although frequently described by travelers, the grandeur of this Volga waterway has never been properly appreciated by English politicians. Within a few short hours' railway ride from St. Petersburg, the Volga can be touched at a navigable point, and from there troops can go in steamers or barges down the Caspian Sea. From the Caspian Sea runs the easy level road from Michaelovsk (near Krasnovodsk) *via* Askabad and Sarakhs, to the gates of Herat and to India.

The resources of the Volga may be gathered from the fact that the traffic on the river amounts to over ten million tons annually, conducted by 650 cargo steamers and 3,000 barges, having the united capacity of nearly 3,000,000 tons. The value of these steamers and barges is estimated at £8,000,000 sterling. In excess of the 3,000 permanent barges of 1,000 tons capacity each, there are hundreds of temporary ones constructed to convey cargoes to Nijni Novgorod, or other destinations, and then broken up. On the Volga and Kama 100 such barges are yearly constructed, with a cargo capacity each of from 300 to 500 tons, and 200 with a capacity of from 5,000 to 8,000 tons. These huge vessels, the size of ocean-going steamers, and the 300-foot permanent barges, are too large to pass through the canal system to the River Neva, the locks of which do not admit the passage of craft exceeding in length 147 feet; hence 1,000 smaller barges, 100 feet long, and having a capacity of 200 or 300 tons apiece, are yearly constructed simply for the transport of goods from the Volga to the Neva. Besides the extensive shipbuilding above referred to, 4,000 barges, wherries, and fishing-boats are annually built on the Volga for the lower course of the river and the Caspian. The central point of the traffic on the Volga is Nijni Novgorod, where there is an annual turn-over at the Great Fair of from twenty to twenty-five millions sterling. Astrakhan, at the mouth, does a trade of £5,000,000 a year. The traffic passing through the mouth of the Volga amounted to a million tons in 1882.

These are some of the transport resources of the river Volga, down which Russia is dispatching troops to re-enforce Komaroff's army at the gates of Herat. Besides the navigable waterway from Tver, the railway system touches the river at four great points— Nijni Novgorod, Samara, Saratoff, and Tsaritzin. To each of these, troops could be dispatched from Middle and Western Russia, and, on their arrival at the river, find plenty of transport to carry them down to the sea.

That sea—the Caspian—associated in most Englishmen's minds with sands and scorpions, is now a great basin of busy commerce. Over 200,000,000 herrings are caught in it every year. The petroleum trade of Baku, opposite Michaelovsk, employs fifty large steamers and hundreds of sailing vessels. Seven thousand vessels enter and leave the port every year. The port of Baku contains pier accommodation for 100 steamers at one and the same time, while the petroleum refineries give the means of drawing largely upon engineering resources. Without experiencing anything like the difficulty she encountered in 1877, Russia could assemble in the magnificent harbor of Baku an army quite as large as she invaded Turkey with then. It would have better transport, the troops would arrive at the base in better trim, and they would have the enormous food supply of the Volga to sustain them in their campaign.

The army of the Caucasus, 100,000 strong on a peace footing, is for the most part concentrated in Transcaucasia. Through Transcaucasia runs a railway from Batoum, on the Black Sea, to this same Baku on the Caspian. Baku, therefore, would serve as the concentrating point of the forces of the Caucasus as well as those from Russia proper.

Baku, which in 1879 only contained 15,000 people, now has a population of 50,000, and is becoming a great city. There are 5,000 houses in the place, and 1,500 shops, and 200 oil refineries turning out a quarter of a million tons of burning oil every year.

Across the water to Michaelovsk is a day's journey; then comes the railway trip to Kizil Arvat terminus, 144 miles inland, where the Transcaspian desert ends, and the fertile country commences, running all the way to Herat. As I have said, the transport power of the Caspian is now such that Russia could rapidly move, not simply thousands of troops, but tens of thousands; for the fifty steamers are new and large, and the hundred sailing vessels ships of great capacity.

We may therefore say, so far as the collection of troops and stores in the Caspian is concerned, Russia could surpass any efforts we could make on the Quetta side of India. But there is another great fact. This assembly could go on secretly, and almost without our knowledge—at least, definite information could be suppressed—while we could not move a soldier from England without the circumstance being known to Russia. Further, while not a soldier could get to India without the liability of being attacked on the way, for Russia might be able to secure allies in Europe, she herself could assemble a vast army in the Caspian, behind the screen of the Caucasus, without having to detach a single man to protect it.

In 1877 Kishineff was the concentrating point from which Russia invaded Turkey. For her troops to proceed to that point, the difficulties of transport and food supply were infinitely greater than they would be from the present terminal point of the Transcaspian railway system at Kizil Arvat. I say present terminal point, because although her engineers have been engaged extending the line since last autumn, nothing is known as to the amount of new railway now open for traffic. Now, from Kishineff to Constantinople, the troops of the Shipka column had to march 750 miles, and of the Sophia column, 970 miles. If we treat Kizil Arvat as a Kishineff, the distance thence to Herat is only 523 miles, as compared with the distances traversed by the Russians in 1877, given above. But perhaps an objection may be raised to treating Kizil Arvat as a Kishineff—then start from the decks of the transports in the Caspian. The distance even then is only 667 miles, as compared with the 1,000 miles many Russians trudged on foot before they got to Constantinople.

And mark this difference. Russia, in invading Turkey, had Austria to threaten her flank. There would be no such enemy in the Caspian. Russia, further, had to cross the Danube—one of the largest rivers in Europe—in face of Turks. She had to encounter large armies at Plevna, and traverse the almost impregnable Balkan range, meeting, on the other side, armies again before she got to Constantinople. In the case of Herat, nothing of the kind exists. There is not a single river of any magnitude the whole distance from the Caspian to Herat. There is no mountain range—only the Paropamisus Downs, containing, according to Gospodin Lessar, at least twenty good crossings. And instead of great armies, the Russians would find no enemy at all the whole way to their present outposts, and could now utilize the 50,000 Turcoman irregular horse to assist them in their undertaking.

Thus the defense of Herat, in the face of such odds, is a very serious matter. It is no permanent advantage to us that the forces at present in the Transcaspian region should be relatively small, compared with the larger invading army I have referred to. Said a Russian general to me, during a conversation at Moscow during the Coronation festivities, " We have now such a good road to the heart of Afghanistan, and the communications with the Caspian base, and from the Caspian base to Askabad, are so perfect, and admit of such a ready movement of troops, that we need only a handful of men to garrison the Turcoman region. It is cheaper to maintain 50,000 men in the Tiflis district than at Geok Tepé and Askabad; and we can throw them from the one point to the other at a moment's notice."

Had Skobeleff been alive to-day, his plan for the invasion of India would have undoubtedly been the massing, on a large scale, of troops in the Caspian basin, and their dispatch to Herat *viâ* the Askabad-Sarakhs road and the parallel one from Astrabad *viâ* Meshed. The second is the old highway of invasion, and runs through the richest districts of Khorassan. On reaching the Hari Rud at Kusan, the Astrabad column would march to the south of Herat, leaving on its left flank the Paropamisus hills, and sever the Afghan fortress from India.

It must not be forgotten that the Russians at Pul-i-Khatun and Zulfikar have only to make three marches to the west, and the occupation of Meshed would provide them at a stroke with resources in transport, food, and supplies generally, equal to those at Herat. Such an occupation might be made by arrangement with the Shah, who is notoriously anti-English, or without it; for if war arose, Russia would not hesitate a moment to cut off Khorassan from Persia at Shahrood, and use the Golden province as a line of advance and base of operations.

Hence the invasion of India, or the smaller operation of an attack on Herat, is an enterprise which seems perfectly feasible to Russian military men, and it is the conviction that the conflict would end in their favor that renders the Russian seizure of the gates of Herat so ominous. If Russia had not felt that she could safely affront this country, she would have never moved a Cossack across the Sarakhs-Khoja-Saleh boundary to the northern pasture lands of the Key of India.

---

## CHAPTER VII.

### THE RUSSIAN RAILWAY TO HERAT AND INDIA.

The advance of the Russian locomotive—Immense changes it will occasion in Central Asia—Inevitable junction of the Indian and European railway systems *viâ* Candahar and Herat—Only £4,000,000 needed to complete the link—Charing Cross to India in nine days—Statistics of the line.

A VERY great factor in the Russo-Indian question is the Transcaspian railway, which is sanctioned for construction as far as Askabad, and, according to Russian reports, is to be afterward continued to Sarakhs. If we allow the Russians to maintain their hold on the gates of Herat, and ourselves subsequently retire from safeguarding the fortress with English officers and troops, it will be always possible, after the place has been carried by a *coup de main*, for Russia to connect it with her railway system in a few months. The menace to India would then be perfect.

To a correspondent of the *Cologne Gazette* Lessar is reported to have said as follows, the second week in March: "People attribute to us the idea of continuing the Transcaspian railway from Askabad to Sarakhs and Herat—a twofold absurdity. I have studied those regions in all directions and am convinced that a line to Herat by Merv must follow the course of the Murghab, for a desert railway must, if possible, keep close to water. From a technical standpoint the railway from Merv to Herat would be easy, for there is a gentle rise, and the chain of mountains, or rather hills, called the Paropamisus, has at least 20 good passes, and its loftiest peak is not 1,000 mèters high. During the Russo-Turkish war I took part in laying down the much more difficult line from Bender to Galatz, and I believe the line from Merv to Herat would scarcely take more than three weeks. I should, however, be the last to recommend such a line. What we require in Central Asia is a line going from Askabad to Merv, and thence north-eastward to Bokhara, so as to connect the markets together, facilitate the exchange of products, and open up new outlets for our Russian industry. When once we were at Herat with our line, the connection with the Indian lines at Quetta would only be a question of time, and then farewell to our dreams of our Central Asian culture and industry. Manchester and Birmingham would soon find their way by Quetta and Herat to Merv, glutting the Bokharan markets with their cheap goods, and we should see that we had merely labored for the English. The line to Herat held up as a bugbear in the English newspapers, is only an imaginary evil for the English, but a real one for us Russians, for so far from implying the entrance of the Russians into India, it would rather imply the entrance of English goods into the Central Asian markets, and no military advantages could guard us against this economic danger."

In interviewing, unless the interviewer knows a little of the subject he is discussing, he is always sure to involve his "subject" in mistakes. Hence it would be unfair, in the present instance, to charge some of the above absurdities to Lessar himself. The interviewer implies that Lessar said that Russia had no idea of running the line to Sarakhs (as well as to Herat), and also puts the matter as though Lessar stated that the railway ought to run from Merv to Herat, not *via* Sarakhs. This, of course, is nonsense. What Lessar meant was that Russia, in pushing the line to Sarakhs and Merv, had no idea of extending it to Herat and India; and he was only saying what was commonplace when he told the interviewer that from Merv to Herat a line must follow the Murghab. Of course he would object to such a line, because it is not on the route to India: the railway ought to turn off at Sarakhs to do that. As for its being possible to make a railway from Merv to Herat in three weeks, that was a statement Lessar could obviously never have made, for the construction of 240 miles of railway is not to be done by any human power at present existing at the rate of eleven or twelve miles a day.

I take notice of this interview at all, simply to point out one or two important facts which are not yet properly appreciated by the British public. In the first place, it is an established fact that can not be in any way contested, that it *is* possible to construct a railway from Askbakad to Herat, and thence to India. Secondly, it is equally beyond dispute that the two railway systems of Russia and India are pushing toward each other in such a manner, that unless one of them suspends the advance, they will be infalliably within a few short hundred miles of each other in a year or two's time. Further, that when this comes about, all that will be needed will be the construction of this short section to unite India with Europe by railway, and provide the world with a rival route to that *via* the Suez Canal. Finally, that as this new route will give Europe the means of getting to India in nine days or so, and India the means of returning the compliment, the traffic passing along the line through Afghanistan to India and back again will set up an amount of local progress and movement, altogether changing the conditions on the Afghan frontier.

Russia, who is the creator of this new route, and who is doing her best to enforce its opening up, is now posing as its opponent, so as to lull England until she seizes Herat. And she selects as the mouthpiece of this opposition the very man who has done more than any one living to bring about the inevitable junction of the Indian and Russian railways!

Before describing the line, let me define what she is doing, and what she is going to do. She is going to build the railway as far as Sarakhs, for that is an admitted fact in Russia, and Lessar himself told me as much a few days after his arrival in London. From Sarakhs, however, she does not mean to push on to Herat or its gates, not because it is impossible or difficult, but because England would regard it as a menace. To allay our uneasiness on this score she says that she is going to turn off from Sarakhs to Merv, and afterward extend the line to Turkestan. Therefore, she asks that we shall not be disturbed by any bugbear of a railway to Herat, but allow her to retain the gates of that place without fear of the locomotive pushing up thither.

It is well we should clearly appreciate the reasons of this attitude. She does not want us rendered more determined to dispossess her of the gates of Herat by the fears excited by the advance of her locomotive, and she does not desire that we ourselves should rush on our Quetta line to Candahar and the Key of India. In her view that would be a calamity. It would strengthen our defense of Herat too much. But it would not do for her to say this; therefore a commercial objection is trotted out, and she expresses a fear that if the two railway systems were joined, England would deluge the markets of Central Asia with her cheap produce.

To my view there is something delightfully audacious in this last contention. It is a well-known fact that every Russian advance means the exclusion of English goods from more markets in Central Asia, and that this is accomplished, not by the establishment of superior transport, but by the short and summary method of ordering our manufactures out of the country altogether. At present no English manufactured goods whatever are allowed to cross the frontier in Central Asia from India; and the produce of India, such as tea, indigo, etc., is subjected to the heaviest duties. The fear expressed by Lessar, therefore, is grotesquely absurd. All that Russia would require to do, on the junction of the Russo-Indian lines, would be to frame an edict and place a custom-house officer at the connecting point, and English commerce with the markets of Turkestan and Turkmenia would be effectually gripped and held in tether. Nobody knows this better than Russia herself.

On this account we must not be lured into surrendering the gates of Herat, because Russia is *only* going to extend the Transcaspian railway to Sarakhs and Merv for the moment. As those two points form the bases of her present position, that simple extension alone would be a most serious matter; because Russia would have her railway system running to within 202 and 240 miles of Herat, while ours at Pishin would be 469 miles distant. It does not need much knowledge of military affairs to appreciate how great an advantage the Russian generals would possess over our own, if no corresponding movement were made by this country.

In this manner the Russian railway advance provokes and compels the advance of the English locomotive into Afghanistan. This is a serious annoyance to Russia, for she wants to get as close to India as she can, and secure as much of the future highway as possible. She would like the junction to take place not further from India than, say, Candahar. She does not want England to push on the line to Herat, and thereby prevent her securing the Key of India. Hence the utmost efforts are being made to allay our fears, and prevent us, when the railway is finished to Pishin, from advancing for the moment any further.

"Don't talk about the Transcaspian railway," said Skobeleff to me in 1882. "That's a fad of Annenkoff's. Nothing will ever come of it."

Yet it has been since revealed in Grodekoff's history of the Turcoman war, that Skobeleff did attach an enormous value to the line, and took the deepest interest in its construction. He realized at the very outset how vastly it would improve the Russian position at the gates of the Key of India.

The notion of a Transcaspian railway did not crop up until after Lomakin's defeat at Geok Tepé in 1879. But for that defeat it is a question whether it would have been constructed at all. The disaster at Geok Tepé shook the power of Russia in Central Asia, and rendered a campaign of revenge unavoidable. The principal difficulty in the second expedition consisted in the scarcity east of the Caspian of transport animals, to convey the stores of the army across the narrow band of desert lying between the Caspian and Kizil Arvat. To overcome this a service of traction engines and *fourgons* was projected by General Petrusevitch, and later on, the construction of a tramway. Ultimately, at the suggestion of General Annenkoff, the Controller of Russian military transport, Skobeleff decided on a regular railway, and induced the Government to send him the 100 miles of railway lying idle in store at Bender.

At first the railway works were meant to be only temporary, but Annenkoff conceiving the idea of some day earning for himself the reputation of a second Lesseps, by pushing on the line to India, and giving the world a new route to the East, made the line so strong that, when at last it was finished to Kizil Arvat, 144 miles from the Caspian, the five-foot metal way was as good as any in Russia.

On Annenkoff's return from the seat of war he issued a pamphlet in support of his idea. This was exposed to a deal of ridicule in Russia, as well as in England; and not only did the Marquis of Hartington pooh-pooh the idea in the House of Commons, but even Sir Henry Rawlinson, Sir Richard Temple, and other so-called "alarmists" put it aside with disdain, as not entering the sphere of practical politics.

On myself, however, the pamphlet made a very different impression. So subversive of the condition of things in Central Asia did it promise to be, in my estimation, that I published a pamphlet on the subject, with a *fac-simile* of Annenkoff's map, and issued 1,000 copies to Parliament and the press. In this pamphlet I demonstrated, by calculations based on Lessar's discoveries, that the extension of the line from Kizil Arvat to Herat would only cost Russia £2,192,000, while the complete junction of the Russian and Indian railway systems could be effected for a little over £6,000,000 sterling.*

Even this failed to move the lethargy of the Government beyond causing the improvement of the Bolan route to be taken in hand, which, I have been informed, was due to this pamphlet; but in Russia it had the fact of dissipating much of the ridicule to which Annenkoff had been exposed by the press, with which he was not popular, and when in 1883 the Transcaucasian railway was finished from Batoum on the Black Sea to Baku on the Caspian, it was at once seen how natural a continuation of this trade route Annenkoff's line was across the Caspian.

Still nothing was done by England as a counterpoise until Merv was annexed. Then the Government, which had stopped the Candahar railway, and literally pitched a part of the line all over the country, gave orders for the same railway to be rushed on with all

---

* "The Russian Railway to Herat and India."

possible speed, and to be carried to the Pishin plateau beyond Quetta.

As soon as this order was given Russia retorted by sanctioning the extension of her own line from Kizil Arvat to Askabad.

In this manner, even if the advance had not subsequently taken place to the gates of Herat, two further sections of the Russo-Indian railway would have been constructed all the same. Whether England will retort on the extension to Askabad by a fresh advance on Candahar remains to be seen. The generality of English politicians assert that it will be absolutely essential if the Russian line be carried on to Sarakhs.

At the outset, let us see how the Russo-Indian line will stand if no further advances be made beyond those actually sanctioned— that is to say, as far as Askabad on the Russian side, and Pishin on the English.

|  | Miles. | Cost per mile. | Total. |
|---|---|---|---|
| Askabad to Sarakhs. ., .......... .. | 185½ ..... | £4,000 | ...... £742,000 |
| Sarakhs to Herat................. | { 102½ .....<br>{ 100 ..... | 4,000 {<br>5,000 } | ...... 910,000 |
| Askabad to Herat........... ...... | 388 miles | .......... | £1,652,000 |

The cost of the line is based upon the calculations of Annenkoff and Lessar. Between Askabad and Sarakhs, according to Lessar, the country is quite flat, and without a single obstacle to a railway. As regards the country from Sarakhs to Herat, Lessar, after his survey in 1882, divided it into two sections. A half, he said, would be as level as the Askabad-Sarakhs district, and the remaining half identical with the country commonly met with in Russia—that is to say, easy to traverse, but less easy than the rest, because of some hills and undulations. I have increased the cost of this by £1,000 a mile. I should say that no one has more insisted upon the feasibility of the line to Herat than Lessar himself, and it is he himself who has selected the Askabad-Sarakhs route as the best from the Caspian.

Thus, for less than the price of a couple of ironclads Russia could carry her railway system right into the very Key of India. Considering that she has just spent £9,000,000 in completing her railway communication between the Caspian and the Black Sea, this is a very insignificant outlay.

On the Indian side, when the Candahar railway was recommenced the terminal point was Sibi, 599 miles from Herat. The sanctioned extension to Pishin will carry the line to within 100 miles of Candahar, or 469 miles of the Key of India. Thus, if we go no further, Russia will be 81 miles nearer Herat with her locomotive than ourselves.

At £5,000 a mile, the estimated cost of the Candahar railway, the outlay on our section to Herat, 469 miles, would be £2,345,000 the country being more difficult between Candahar and Herat than between Askabad and Sarakhs. In this manner, when the sanctioned extensions are finished, all the expenditure that will be needed to establish through communication between Europe and India by railway will be less than £4,000,000 sterling.

|  | Miles. | | Cost or Section. |
|---|---|---|---|
| Askabad to Herat | 388 | | £1,652,000 |
| Pishin to Herat | 469 | | 2,345,000 |
| Total length and cost | 857 | | £3,997,000 |

Considering the revolution that would be accomplished by the possibility of proceeding from Charing Cross to India in nine days, this outlay is, relatively, an absurd trifle. If no political considerations hindered its accomplishment, a company might be formed and the money raised in London for the railway in a few hours.

At the present moment Russia is going to spend, in extending the Vladikavkaz railway to the Caspian and Black Sea, a sum of money nearly equal to that which I have given above as all that is needed to render it possible for English people to proceed to India in nine days. When this Vladikavkaz line is finished it will still further improve the proposed line of communications. At present the route would be Calais, Berlin, Odessa, Batoum, Baku, Michaelovsk, Askabad, Herat, Candahar, and Pishin; the water-breaks being from Dover to Calais, Odessa to Batoum, and Baku to Michaelovsk. When, however, the Vladikavkaz line is completed the water-breaks will be only two. The traveler will proceed direct from Calais to Petrovsk, on the Caspian, and cross over thence to Michaelovsk, thus saving the journey across the Black Sea. This Vladikavkaz-Petrovsk link will be completed next year, so that by the time the Afghan railway is open the line of steam communication from London to Calcutta, viâ Herat, will be perfect throughout.

I have said that in Russia it is stated on the best authority that a decision has already been arrived at to push on the Transcaspian Railway, when finished to Askabad, still further, to Sarakhs. This has been practically confirmed by Lessar. Whether it will turn off then to Merv or not we need not discuss. I do not believe it will. I am persuaded Russia will make a dash then for Herat. But let us simply accept Russia's admission that the line will cease advancing toward India when it attains Sarakhs. Even if she goes no further, one thing is already certain—England will inevitably push on her Pishin line to Candahar.

You may possibly think that events are not likely to be ripe for some time to come for a return to Candahar; but every hour they are tending to an English occupation of Herat, and, whether the communications be maintained through Candahar or not, the connection between Herat and Pishin will inevitably take the form of a railway. If Russia pushes on her locomotive to Sarakhs, to within 202 miles of Herat, it will not do for our locomotive to be 469 miles short of it. Public opinion will compel the Government to push on the Indian railway system to Candahar.

In that case, the position will be this:

|  | Miles. | | Total cost. |
|---|---|---|---|
| Sarakhs to Herat | 202½ | | £910,000 |
| Candahar to Herat | 369 | | 1,845,000 |
| Total length and cost | 571½ | | £2,755,000 |

Thus, whether Russia turns off afterward to Merv or not, the extension of her railway system to Sarakhs will have the effect of reducing the gap between the railways of Europe and India to less than 600 miles. But I do not believe that the public would be satisfied with this state of affairs. Relatively the Russian locomotive would be far too close to Herat, and consequently our Candahar line would be pushed on absolutely to Herat. This done, the gap would be reduced to a paltry 200 miles, and there can be hardly a doubt that the moment a period of peace ensued the pressure of commerce would quickly bring about a junction.

Hence, I hold that in a very few years' time India and Europe will be joined together by a quick route of railway running through Herat, and the traffic speeding along it, even if it be only passenger, will revolutionize the Russo-Indian region, and efface the southern portion of the Afghan barrier.

If it be urged that I am too sanguine, I reply that the changes I prognosticate are nothing compared with what has been accomplished since 1880. Take Merv. It was then as mysterious as Timbuctoo, and common report affirmed that it was instant death for any European to penetrate to the haunt of the man-stealing Turcomans. To-day, the postman goes his rounds in the oasis, the policeman guards the shops in the bazaar, and a site is already staked off for a permanent telegraph office. Take Herat. Less than eighteen months ago no Englishman thought of the Sepoy and Cossack confronting each other on the Paropamisus slopes. Herat was as much out of the world, so far as European intercourse was concerned as the Arctic region. To-day some of its gates are in the Postal Union, and a post-card can be sent by Lessar from London to Alikhanoff at Pul-i-Khisti for a penny.

Strange as it may seem, the opening up of this short cut to India, on the importance of which I have been insisting for years, without having produced much effect on the British public, is nothing more than a revival of a scheme that excited a mania in England 150 years ago. The Russians are only trying to do to-day what the English sought to accomplish in the reign of George II.

One hundred and fifty years ago the merchants of England were bitten with the idea of establishing trade relations with India via Russia and the Caspian Sea. The goods were to be conveyed to St. Petersburg or some other Baltic port; they were then to be sent by canal or road to the upper course of the Volga, and they were afterward to float down the river 2,000 miles in barges to its mouth. Here they were to be placed on ships and taken to Astrabad Bay, and from this point dispatched by caravan through Persia and Afghanistan to India.

If the conditions of trade and travel in Russia at the time could be adequately realized, people would be amazed at the wonderful enterprise of these merchants. In the Baltic there was constant war, the Volga swarmed with pirates, the Caspian was a Persian lake with rapine and disorder seething round its shores, and the whole of the country thence to India was as turbulent and untamed as the worst parts of Afghanistan to-day. Finally, in India itself, France was still the stronger power, and Clive had not commenced the career of conquest destined to convert the country into the magnificent dependency of the Empire we find it to-day. Such were a few of the conditions of the time the Russia Company sought to open up the Transcaspian route to India. In the interval that has elapsed the English, who only held a few points on the east coast of India (excluding the then insignificant port, without territory, of Bombay), have moved toward Europe from Calcutta to Quetta 2,000 miles. The whole of this country they have conquered and organized, and railway communication runs right through it, or will do so when the Pishin railway is finished. The Russians, on their part, whose final stronghold was Astrakhan, have advanced toward India as far as Ak Robat and other gates of Herat, or 1,200 miles, the entire length of which is open to trade, and the greater portion traversed by steam communication.

In this manner, instead of the Russians at Astrakhan and the English at Calcutta being over 3,700 miles apart from one another, and exercising no control over the intervening country, as was the case when Jonas Hanway tried to push English goods to India 150 years ago, they are now, measuring from the Russian position at Ak Robat to the English at Pishin, only a little over 500 miles apart, while some of their soldiers face each other. Yet, forgetful of the past, and blind to the forces at work at the present, English statesmen for years have been acting as though the trumpery Afghan barrier were destined to last for centuries.

## CHAPTER VIII.

### THE FUTURE OF THE AFGHAN BARRIER.

Impossibility of maintaining the Afghan barrier as it is—The Sepoy must confront the Cossack—The expansion of Russia—Will Russia let us garrison Herat?—Skobeleff's Afghan programme—England must herself organize the Afghan frontier, and man it with troops.

THE Czar rules 100 million subjects; the Queen controls in India 250 millions. Between the two empires lies the Afghan barrier.

What is the Afghan barrier? To the majority of Englishmen it is a vast mountainous region, extremely inaccessible, and peopled throughout with fierce tribes averse to any intercourse with the Feringhi. To conquer it would be a task equal to the Russian conquest of the Caucasus. To attempt commercial intercourse would be to expose England to the risk of having to perpetually avenge brutal murders. For Russia to try to march an army into any part of the Ameer's dominions would be to involve her in those disasters and losses which marked our last Afghan War. If given to strife among themselves, the people are welded together by a common feeling of patriotism against the attacks of outsiders. Irreclaimably cruel, they are best let alone; and even if Russia tore her way through the tribesmen, and broke the Ameer's levies, England could confront the wearied and mauled invaders in the Khyber and Bolan Passes, and effectually check an inrush into India.

Thus, to the view of most Englishmen, Afghanistan is a material as well as a moral barrier. To my view it is neither.

There is only one possible solution of the Central Asian Question.

If the Russian advance is to be permanently arrested, we must confront the Cossack with the Sikh. Unless we move up to Russia, Russia will move down upon India. There can be no permanent zone maintained between the two empires.

We shall see what a breakable barrier this Afghanistan is, if we look at a few plain facts plainly. All I ask, as the outset, is that you look at them with your own eyes, and not through the spectacles of 1842 or 1878; nor yet, again, through the lenses of political old fogies, or, worse still, of mere party hacks, who, because they or their leaders expressed such and such opinions—five, ten, or twenty years ago—would rather see the empire perish than change them.

The Russians are posted at the gates of Herat; the English are posted on the hills dominating the avenues to Candahar. Between them lies the Afghan barrier.

That barrier, physically, is of such a character, that the Russians could drive a four-in-hand from their own Cossack outposts to ours, and, during the 549 miles' ride, they would pass only two towns on the road—Herat with 50,000, and Candahar with 60,000 people. There are bad roads in Afghanistan, but they do not lie between the Russians and the English. There are fierce tribes, but they lie the thinnest between the Czar's soldiers and the Queen's. There are patriotic Afghans, but the least sentimental and the most amenable to European influence, lie between the Cossack and the Sikh. There are fearful mountains, but they do not lie along the road I mention. Horrible deserts exist, but in this case the most fertile parts of Afghanistan mark the route. In one word, there is no barrier at all between the Russians and the English, except such as we ourselves may try and create, and interpose to check the advance of the Cossack.

Let me put the matter more plainly in the shape of a parable.

A certain man stood at the junction of two roads: one, a level railway, along which, in the distance, could be seen a locomotive advancing, and the other a winding post road which disappeared over a lofty hill. Seeing him standing on the metals, people shouted to the man to beware of the advancing train. But the man refused to look along the line; he kept his gaze fixed on the old post road, and replied, "I can see no stage-coach coming over the mountain: I don't believe in your warnings." And so he stood obstinately on the metals, refusing to move, until the train came up and cut him to pieces.

Such has been the attitude of England and her statesmen in regard to the Russian advance upon India. That advance was formerly through Orenburg and the deserts of Central Asia. When English statesmen looked in those days toward the advancing Cossack, they gazed at Cabul and the lofty Hindoo Koosh in its rear. There *was* a barrier then. But since 1869 the Russians have been advancing in another direction. They have been rattling along the almost level road from the Caspian to Candahar. Still, with woful perversity, English statesmen have refused to divert their gaze from the old mountain road, and have kept looking at Cabul, when they ought to have been watching Herat. To-day, they are beginning to glance in the right direction, but unless they rid themselves of all the old-fashioned notions about the Afghans and the Afghan barrier, the Russians will smash their way into India.

In discussing the Russo-Indian question, politicians frequently quote the opinions expressed by Wellington in 1842, and by Law-rence and others in 1860–70, when Russia was conquering the deserts of Turkestan. They might just as well quote the Talmud. All the conditions have changed since those opinions were expressed; everything has been turned topsy-turvy in Afghanistan and Central Asia, and the authorities cited for passing party purposes by shal-low politicians would be the first to disown the erroneous application of these opinions if they were alive to-day.

To the Russian official or officer who has made the journey of 3,000 miles to get from St. Petersburg to the gates of Herat, what is the trumpery 549 miles of easy road intervening between him and the Pishin outposts! The Herat-Candahar-region may be a barrier to politicians who have passed their lives in babble and barleycorn measurements, but to Russians, accustomed to think no more of a thousand miles' journey than the Londoner does of a 'bus ride to the Bank, the distance separating the Cossack from India is grotesquely insignificant.

The defect of the Afghan barrier is this—that it is weakest where it ought to be most strong; and we can only remedy that defect by taking the organization of the defense into our own hands. In plainer words, we ourselves must hold the gates of Herat.

All discussions about the return to Candahar are beside the mark. We can occupy Candahar whenever we like, and we need not con-cern ourselves about its security. The whole of our efforts must be concentrated upon the safeguarding of Herat.

We must make sure of the bulwarks of Afghanistan. The ques-tion of the inner defenses can be settled at our leisure afterward.

To hear some people talk, the installation of an Indian garrison at Herat would appear to be the most difficult task that has ever tested the resources of our empire. As a matter of fact, the army con-centrated at Pishin would simply have to march 400 odd miles to get to Herat, and that by a broad wagon road. To a nation that has just sent, in face of fearful obstacles, a force from Cairo to Khartoum (1,500 miles), such an expedition should be relatively a common-place enterprise. Ten thousand Indian troops, aided by tribal levies, would be all that would be needed for the moment to safeguard the Key of India. The real difficulty consists, not in getting those troops there, but in making sure that Russia will not issue an ulti-matum forbidding their advance.

It may be opportune to repeat what transpired during a discussion I had with Professor Martens on the subject in 1882. The connec-tion of Professor Martens with the Russian Foreign Office is well known, and some of his utterances appeared to me, at the time, so fraught with warning that I printed them in italics. I give the con-versation and my comment just as I published it in 1882,* and I think it will be found to possess significance of an undoubted char-acter at the present moment.

* "The Russian Advance toward India: Conversations with Russian States-men and Generals on the Central Asian Question, page 207."

The conversation was upon the features of Afghanistan.  I mentioned that General Annenkoff had said, " 'Take Afghanistan, for sake of peace.' "

" But Professor Martens declared that England would not be able to annex Afghanistan *without Russia's permission*, or as he more delicately put it, ' without informing her first of her intentions;' *while as to Herat, he said that Russia would view an English occupation of the place with displeasure.*

" He would not allow that we enjoyed supremacy in Afghanistan; nor yet that we could regard it as a second Bokhara.  He said Afghanistan was an independent State, and a neutral one; and, with reference to Lord Hartington's declaration last year, ' that England would not allow any power to interfere with the internal and external affairs of Afghanistan,' which I quoted, to show what our Government thought of Russian pretensions, he said that the declaration was contrary to the views which Russia and England diplomatically expressed upon the matter, previous to the Marquis's speech.  He would not agree that the Afghan war had canceled those views.  ' Herat,' he said, ' is quite as important to Russia as to England.  If it is the Key of India it is also the Key of Central Asia.  If we were there we could threaten you in India; if you were there you could threaten us in Central Asia.'          .

" This opinion was expressed also by Baron Jomini, one of the Under-Secretaries of State at the Russian Foreign Office, to Lord Dufferin in 1879.  Writing on July 16th in that year, he states that Baron Jomini said to him: ' Although we don't intend to go to Merv, or to do anything which may be interpreted as a menace to England, you must not deceive yourself, for the result of our present proceedings ' (*i.e.*, the operations of General Lazareff for conquering and annexing Akhal) ' *will be to furnish us with a base of operations against England hereafter, should the British Government, by the occupation of Herat, threaten* ' our present position in Central Asia.'

" Professor Martens would not admit that Herat was as much a part of Afghanistan as Cabul or Candahar, and thought that Persia ought to have it.  On my pointing out what a rotten State Persia was, and how completely it was under Russian control, he said that if Russia occupied Herat she would make Persia her enemy.  My strong dissent from this led him to propose that Herat should be made into a sort of Switzerland, on the buffer State system, although he had previously expressed his disbelief in the possibility of keeping up Afghanistan as a buffer between the two empires.  I held that such a project was impossible with Asiatics, but he continued to maintain that England should keep her hands off the place under any contingencies

" As I gathered from him, he maintains Russia's right to annex all the territory up to the Afghan frontier, if the nomads provoke her to advance; he holds that Russia should also have Afghan Turkestan—*i.e.*, the country between the Oxus and the Hindoo Koosh.  He considers that Herat ought not to be treated as an Afghan possession, and, finally, he insists that the rest of Afghanistan should be looked upon as a neutral independent State, in the existence of which Russia has as much interest as England.  It is needless to

4

point out that these opinions can not but be so many red rags to English Russophobists, and that, much as the Professor desires a reconciliation between England and Russia, a cessation of the Central Asian agitation is impossible while they are maintained. I myself would allow Russia to annex up to Afghanistan; but I would give her to understand that that country is English territory, and must not be looked upon as less our property than Mysore or Baroda.

"I used to think that the claims put forward by the *Golos* and *Novoe Vremya*, asserting Russia's right to treat Afghanistan as a neutral State, and Herat as apart from Afghanistan, were merely expressions of Anglophobe feeling. It has surprised me to find them seriously maintained by a person of such weight as Professor Martens."

Since Russia seized the gates of Herat, the St. Petersburg press has repeatedly intimated that she would not allow us to occupy and garrison the Key of India. These opinions have been treated somewhat heedlessly by the English press. They have regarded them simply as ravings of irresponsible journalists. But knowing what I do of the aims of Russian statesmen, and with the warnings of Professor Martens ringing in my ears, I can not but think that the threats of the Russian press possess a very serious significance. In my mind I am persuaded, that if we allow this frontier complication to simmer until Russia masses at Sarakhs and Merv and the gates of Herat a more powerful army than Lumsden and the Afghans control for the defense of the Key of India, she will suddenly throw off the mask and deny our right to send a force thither. Hence, if there is to be any advance for the defense of Herat, it must be done without delay.

The present complications are something more than an obstinate controversy about a few miles of frontier. The conviction has been deepening in Russia for years that the economical depression to which it is a prey can only be dissipated by a solution of the Eastern Question, and that that solution is only attainable by taking up such a position on the Indian confines as shall compel England to acquiesce in the Russian occupation of Armenia and Constantinople.

Apparently, Russia has now accepted in full the policy of General Skobeleff, which, published piecemeal since his death, has permeated the army and exercised an extraordinary effect in preparing Russia for fresh sacrifices. Let me quote what Skobeleff wrote to a Russian diplomatist after his return from Geok Tepe, during a rest he was taking on his estate at Spasskoe Selo:

"The expedition of 1880–81, intrusted to me, gave birth to the indispensability of creating new relations with Merv, Afghanistan, and Persia. It rests beyond doubt that the late Emperor would not allow any other influence on the Persian frontier but that of Persia. Let us hope that those high ideals which lay at the foundation of the late Sovereign's programme will remain the leading ones of the present policy. Up to now, our national misfortunes, according to our view, have mainly arisen, not from the breadth of our ideas, but from the irresolution and changeableness of our political and ideal aim of operations. This want of determination, hand in hand with financial unscrupulousness, has lain a heavy burden on the whole structure of the State. Personally, for me the whole Central Asian question is fully palpable and clear. If by the aid of it we do not decide in a comparatively short time to take in hand seriously the Eastern Question—that is, to dominate the Bosphorus—the fleece is not worth the tanning. Sooner or later, Russian statesmen will have to acknowledge that Russia must rule the Bosphorus. That on this depends not only her greatness as a power of the first magnitude, but also her security in a defensive sense, and the corresponding development of her manufacturing centers and trade. Without a serious demonstration in the direction of India, in all probability on the side of Candahar, a war for the Balkan peninsula is not to be thought of. It is indispensable to maintain in Central Asia, *at the gates* of the corresponding theater of war, a powerful body of troops, fully equipped and seriously mobilized. We might give up the whole of Central Asia in return for a serious and profitable alliance with England, until we had secured those results on the Bosphorus above mentioned, since the whole of Central Asia possesses for Russia only a temporary political significance. As a vestibule to the theater of war in the event of sharp complications, similar to those of 1878, *the conquered Akhal country would serve in conjunction with the exclusive preponderating influence we enjoy in Persia.* . . . With the pacification of the Akkhal Tekke oasis, the widest field of action has opened before Russian influence in Afghanistan, whenever circumstances require it. Examining the strategical roads for the manifestation of this influence, in dependence on the results accruing to England from the Afghan war, we are bound to come to the conclusion that the principal line of operations will rest upon the newly-conquered oasis. The late Emperor, in appointing me commander against the Turcomans, was pleased to declare, in expressing an opinion as to what would be the results of a successful termination of the expedition, that he would not allow on the Persian confines any other preponderating influence except that of Russia. Remembering the sacred words of the Emperor, I hastened forward to Askabad and proposed that the Atak should be vassal to us, and Residents appointed at Meshed, Herat, and Merv; and finally, in drawing the frontier, I considered as a *minimum* of our demands that we should control the mountain passes. . . . What has been said above by me does not constitute a new question, but luckily the success of the Akhal Tekke expedition practically opens to us the possibility of exercising an influence on the pliancy of Great Britain in the event of fresh complications arising from the Eastern Question. This affair, more than any other undertaking, demands knowledge and prolonged systematic preparations. In support of what I have stated, I am happy that I can quote an extract from the reports of Ellis, the English Embassador at Teheran (the contemporary of Simonitch), to Lord Palmerston in 1835, now just published: ' I have arrived at the deep conviction that the British Government can not in any case allow the extension of the dominion of Persia in the direction of Afghanistan without absolutely infringing the security of our Indian possessions. Persia either does not wish, or can not enter into a lasting alliance with Great Britain. Our policy for the future ought consequently to be to regard Persia not as a rampart protecting India, but as a first parallel, from which at a given moment an invasion of India might proceed. Every step of Persia toward the East brings Russia closer to the gates of India.' Here is a revelation to us of political ideas, which ought to lie in the future at the fundament, and with which I was guided in all my operations, both military as well as those concerning the political frontier line of the newly subjugated country.''

This was published in the *Novoe Vremya* last year, on the second anniversary of Skobeleff's death. The gaps in the letter represent portions prudently suppressed by that paper. It if be carefully read, it will be found to possess fuller significance, and contain a more direct bearing on the present Russian advance and the present claims, than anything ever published in the Russian language, including the stale but often quoted will of Peter the Great.

" Russia does not want India; she wants the Bosphorus." Such was the declaration of General Soboleff in the *Russ* a few months ago, and it will be seen that his words represent very neatly the views of Skobeleff. The terms of peace seem simple, and there are certain simple-minded sentimentalists who are carried away by the plausibility of the O. K. and urge that the British lion should lie down with the Russian bear and surrender Constantinople. But I think I shall be able to show that the offer is totally hollow, and one which can not accepted, even by the most willing Russophile.

In the first place, not a single Russian writer has yet defined what the acquisition of " Constantinople " really means. Only one thing is certain—Russia does not mean Constantinople itself and nothing more. On the contrary, she wants the whole of the Bosphorus and Dardanelles to give her a free and uncontrolled passage to the Mediterranean, and the amount of territory she would require with the channels she leaves open. Now, on the north side of the Bosphorus and Dardanelles is European Turkey, nearly as large as Great Britain, with 5,275,000 souls (we exclude East Roumelia and simply reckon the territory under the direct sway of the Porte); and on the south side is Turkey in Asia, larger than Germany, France and Austria combined, with a population of 17,000,000. How much of this would Russia want? Because, having secured the Bosphorus, we know that she would require plenty of territory on both sides to protect it from attack.

As regards territory in Europe, Russia has expressed pretty plainly her desire to take over all that is left of the Porte's dominions, while, in respect to Asia, it is considered essential that she should have Armenia, so as to connect Kars with the Bosphorus. Thus, although the 8,000,000 people in the immediate vicinity of the Bosphorus, and the 14,000,000 other subjects of the Sultan located further off, do not ask for Russian rule, England is requested to surrender the larger portion of them, because Russia wants an outlet to the Mediterranean. On the same grounds Denmark ought also to be surrendered, because the Danes control the exit from the Baltic. Nay, there is greater reason for this, because, while the annexation of Denmark would affect the interests of only 2,000,000 people, the annexation of Constantinople would interfere directly with the destinies of at least 8,000,000 people, and indirectly with 14,000,-000 more. In a word, there can be no Russian acquisition of Constantinople that does not carry with it the annexation of a large proportion of the Sultan's territory, and it is well, therefore, that this should be clearly borne in mind by those who advocate a bargain between Russia and England.

But, supposing England did surrender Constantinople, would India be ever free from attack, as Soboleff implies? Could we safely leave the gates of Herat in Russia's hands? These are questions to which it is impossible to return an affirmative reply.

In the first place, Russia's guarantee, verbal or in writing, would be no guarantee whatever. To rely upon any diplomatic compact would be to put ourselves in a position as bad as that of the suburban policeman, who should hand over in a dark lane his truncheon and revolver to the captured burglar, in return for the scoundrel's assurance to go quietly to the station. It is not England's fault, but Russia's, that there is no guarantee Russia can give us which we can possibly respect. But even if we could place more reliance on Russian treaties, the expansion of Russia is a factor that would infallibly render them in time waste paper. Russia has a frontier line across Asia 5,000 miles in length, no single spot of which can be regarded as permanent. Starting from the Pacific we find that she hankers for the northern part of Corea, regards as undetermined by boundary with Manchuria and Mongolia, regrets that she gave back Kuldja, hopes that she will some day have Kashgar, questions the Ameer's right to rule Afghan Turkestan, demands the gates of Herat, keeps open a great and growing complication with Persia about the Khorassan frontier, treats more and more every year the Shah as a dependent sovereign, discusses having some day a port in the Persian Gulf, and believes she will be the future mistress of the whole of Asia Minor. It may not be Russia's fault that her frontier is nowhere in a condition of rest. I will not discuss that point, but I do insist that the frontier is one which must expand in the future, and in so doing, frequently press on our interests. Consequently, the surrender of Constantinople would be of no avail in bringing about a permanent peace between the two countries, because there exist a score of other loopholes for quarreling between them.

It is the recognition, the sorrowful recognition of this, that renders me such a resolute opponent of the Russian advance into Afghanistan. Were I convinced that the surrender of Constantinople would put an end to the conflict between the two empires, I should be the strongest advocate of such a concession, for I like Russia. I have many sincere friends in the country. I take the deepest interest in its progress and expansion, and I should be the last to advocate war. But I recognize that permanent peace can not be purchased by any surrender, and it is the consciousness that the concessions will only beget fresh demands that causes me to insist on the necessity for resisting to the utmost Russia's claim to the gates of Herat.

However disagreeable the task may be, England has but one course open to her. She must insist on the surrender of the Afghan points seized, and she must apply herself resolutely to the organization of the new frontier. Fortunately, if the Afghan barrier lies open to Russia, it lies open equally to ourselves. The conditions at Herat are totally different from those at Cabul. The people are almost devoid of fanaticism, they have a traditional feeling in our favor, and have already developed a fraternal sentiment since the presence of the Lumsden mission in their midst. Thus, if by friendly arrangement with the Ameer we could maintain a force in or near Herat, the measure would be very popular in the locality.

As regards the actual frontier the matter is still easier. Along the whole valley of Herat to Kusan, the people dwelling in the villages are quiet and well-disposed; north of them, to the Russian outposts, there are scarcely any inhabitants at all. Thus our outposts would be safe on the Hari Rud side of Herat. With regard to the Murghab, immediately north of Herat, are the Jemshidis. These I have already described as peaceful and friendly; so again are the Sarik Turcomans.

Now for Afghan Turkestan. From Bala Murghab to the Oxus the Uzbegs are described by Grodekoff as particularly peaceful—too much so, he thinks, as they thereby expose themselves to Afghan tyranny. The few Turcomans also found are likewise free from turbulence. In this manner a very slight Anglo-Afghan cordon would suffice to guard the frontier from Persia to the Oxus, and it would effectually check Russian designs on Balkh and other fore-posts of the Hindoo Koosh, as well as screen Herat.

To the east of Herat are the Hazaras, and south-east the Amaks. These are supposed to number collectively 650,000 souls, and could supply 20,000 or 30,000 horse equal to the Turcomans. They are Mongols by stock, and so independent that the Afghans have never been able to bring the former totally under subjection. With both, good relations have been established by Sir Peter Lumsden, and it is not anticipated by our Indian military experts that they would occasion any trouble, while, being a non-Afghan people, they would be a valuable support to our cordon, in the event of any tumult among the Afghans themselves. The Firuzkuhis, 80,000 in number, are another tribe that might render excellent assistance.

Thus, a cordon established along the new frontier would have powerful support in its rear, and from Herat to the Oxus would be safe from tribal attack and separated by the Hindoo Koosh from the tumults and fanaticism of Cabul. The sole difficulty is the linking of this cordon with our position at Quetta.

The first thing to be remembered is, that we are the practical proprietors of the whole of Beluchistan, the present Government having established a protectorate over it. It is very important to bear this in mind, because it gives us the means of establishing communication with Herat, without touching Candahar. As a matter of fact, the cordon I have referred to could be extended along the Perso-Afghan frontier to East Beluchistan, and there join hands with our own military forces. It has been pointed out by the highest authority that a railway to Herat is feasible from the port of Gwadur, on the coast of Beluchistan, and this could be carried up to the Key of India without meddling with Candahar, or traversing any country held in force by hostile tribes.

Before Sir Peter Lumsden left England I discussed with him this plan, which I had been maturing some time, and had only refrained from making public to prevent Russia taking timely steps to frustrate it. I based its success upon the tranquil character of the North-west and West Afghan frontiers, and my views on this point

have since been confirmed by the correspondence dispatched from
that region to the English and Indian press.   Such a cordon would
effectually check any further Russian advance, and it would leave
untouched Cabul and Candahar, and the districts generally of
Afghanistan where fanaticism abounds, and the ill-feeling engen-
dered by the last war has not yet passed away.

Of late it has become known that some such plan had been drawn
up by the ablest military authorities in India during the viceroyalty

LORD DUFFERIN.

of the Marquis of Ripon.  I can not help thinking that England's
power in India would have been stronger to-day, had he attended
to this more, and left alone such fire-brand questions as the Ilbert
Bill.

Still, it is not too late for its adoption, if it be taken in hand before Russia consolidates her position at the gates of Herat.   If it be
left untouched till then, Russia, I am persuaded, will never allow
the English to garrison the North-west Afghan frontier without

making a determined effort to prevent it.   On this account, it is essential that public opinion in this country should be perfectly ripe
for the permanent manning of the Afghan frontier with Indian
troops, and that Russia should feel that Earl Dufferin is backed up,
if he adopts such a policy, by the patriotic feeling of the entire English empire.

I may add that our military resources in India are quite equal to
the task, if increased by a few re-enforcements from home, and that
the sole obstacle is, whether the Government may not hold back,
fearing that public opinion in England is not sufficiently advanced
for such a forward movement.   To go into full-details of the policy
would be to lengthen out a book already sufficiently long, and, what
is worse, perhaps lead to Russian intrigue, in London and on the
spot, to prevent its realization.   But I have said enough in this
volume in describing the new frontier, to indicate its feasibility; and
India being ready to take the task in hand, in conjunction with the
Ameer, I venture to express a hope that every reader will do his
utmost to support the authorities at home and in India in accomplishing it.

With regard to Earl Dufferin, little fear need be entertained that
he will prove unequal to the situation.   The case, however, is
different with the Government at home.   Mr. Gladstone's Cabinet
is notoriously given to making concessions, and Russia, well aware
of this, is resorting to every artifice to squeeze it.   Against this evil
tendency must be maintained a determined struggle.   " No surrender!" must be the motto of every Englishman as regards Penjdeh,
and " Hands off!" in respect to Ak Robat, Pul-i-Khisti, and other.
gates of the Key of India.   Whether Russia shall win the great camping-ground of Herat or be permanently excluded from it, depends
largely upon you.   If you, as one of the public, do not manifest a
fixed determination to keep Russia out of Herat and its gates, the
Government will catch the spirit of your indifference, and Russia
will succeed in realizing her demands.

Let me make the appeal, therefore, that if you thoroughly appreciate the importance of preserving Herat, you will not simply
content yourself with silent acquiescence.   The press and the plat-
form are open to you to give publicity to your support, and if you
have means you can help in the dissemination of pamphlets to keep
alive public feeling to the danger of the Russian advance.   I have
never rejected any one's co-operation in the sacred task of safeguarding India from the menace from the North, and gratefully place on
record the encouragement which has been given to my efforts by the
sympathy conveyed to me by my readers.   With your help I may
be able to do more than I am doing; without it I remain just as determined as ever not to allow Russia to have Herat while my tongue
and my pen can prevent it.

England has no aggressive aims in Central Asia; she has no desire to meddle with anybody beyond the Afghan border.   Afghanistan itself she strongly wishes should remain independent, and to
render it so she has been paying the Ameer a subsidy of £120,000 a
year to consolidate his authority.   With that independence I am as
little disposed to meddle as any member of the Manchester school
can be, but I hold that it can never be preserved by the simple proc-

ess of tossing £10,000 a month across our Indian frontier, and exercising no control over its expenditure. The Ameer, if a clever man in some respects, is not everywhere in his dominions a popular sovereign, and only Englishmen who are ignorant of Afghan affairs, or refuse to watch them, can deny that there is only one step between his rule and anarchy. If he were to die to-morrow we have no guarantee that a period of turbulence would not prevail at Cabul, and Russia has pretty plainly informed us that if we do not maintain order throughout Afghanistan, she will not bind herself not to advance across the border to restore it. In other words, an outbreak at Herat would be a sufficient excuse for the occupation of the Key of India.

Again, if Englishmen are blind to the fact, Russia is not, that the tribal differences existing in Afghanistan render the country peculiarly well adapted for gradual disintegration. The notion of a united Afghanistan is fit only for the nursery. The Afghans are conquerors and foreigners in the whole of the country north of the Hindoo Koosh, from Balkh to Herat. Their control of Herat, as Russia is constantly reminding us, is quite of recent origin, and even yet they have not succeeded in imposing their rule over all the clans dwelling between Herat and Cabul. If Russia retains her present position, she will be admirably placed for intriguing with the non-Afghan peoples, and detaching them one by one from the Ameer's rule. The Jemshidis would be operated upon first, then the Uzbegs, afterward the Hazaraks and Aimaks, and so on, with very little trouble. Unless we screen these tribes by an Indian cordon, Russia will be able to eat her way into the heart of Afghanistan.

The rampart of the Sulieman range is as much a delusion as the Paropamisus hills. It used to be thought that a great mountain barrier ran parallel with the Indus, and that it was only pierced by three or four cracks—the Khyber, Bolan, and Gomul passes. That myth was exploded during the last war, a regular survey having disclosed the existence of 289 passes, every one capable of being traversed by camels. In the Dera Ismail Khan district alone there are 92 passes; and in excess of the 289 already mapped on the Indo-Afghan frontier, there are 75 more, leading from Beluchistan into India. To control all these passes in time of war, against an army located at Candahar, would be impossible. Among military men to-day there is no difference of opinion that we must go forward and take up a strong position to control the few roads debouching in the direction of this range. In other words, we must assume charge of the Key of India.

England has to face this fact, and it is no use shirking it. If she does not pervade Afghanistan Russia will, and the weakest part of the barrier being precisely that which is closest to Komaroff and Alikhanoff, there is obviously every facility for the slow sapping intrigue, at which Russia is such an adept. We have already ourselves broken the isolation of Afghanistan by dispatching officers and troops to Herat. Let us develop that intercourse, and upon it base the erection of such a barrier along the Russo-Afghan frontier as will effectually secure Afghanistan from the corroding influence of Russia, and afford a means of consolidating our own. There need be no serious annexations, no meddling with the susceptibilities or power of Ameer or Afghan. Once such a defense is organized, in the Ameer's name, for the Key of India, we can rapidly put in order India itself. But, it must be clearly understood, this can be done only by ousting Russia from the gates of Herat she has seized, and by peremptorily rejecting her demands for the remainder. Otherwise a wedge will have been successfully driven in from Merv and Sarakhs to the great camping-ground of Herat, and it will require an enormous expenditure to defend the broken frontier from such treacherous *coups de main* as the recent seizure of Merv and the dash to the bulwarks of the Key of India.

THE END.

ADVERTISEMENTS.

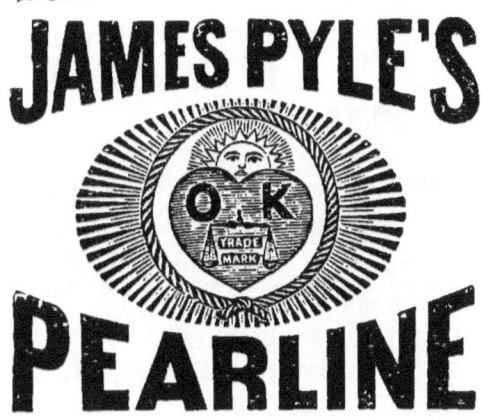

# JAMES PYLE'S PEARLINE

**THE BEST** Washing Compound **EVER INVENTED.**

No Lady, Married or Single, Rich or Poor, Housekeeping or Boarding, will be without it after testing its utility.

Sold by all first-class Grocers, but beware of worthless imitations.

MUNRO'S PUBLICATIONS.

# The Seaside Library
## POCKET EDITION.

II., each .......... 20
279 Little Goldie. By Mrs. Sumner Hayden ........ 20
284 Doris. By "The Duchess" .......... 10
286 Deldee; or, The Iron Hand. By F. Warden ........ 20
330 May Blossom; or, Between Two Loves. By Margaret Lee .......... 20
345 Madam. By Mrs. Oliphant .......... 20
359 The Water-Witch. By J. Fenimore Cooper .......... 20
362 The Bride of Lammermoor. By Sir Walter Scott .. 20

For sale by all newsdealers, or will be sent to any address, postage free, on receipt of 12 cents for single numbers, and 25 cents for double numbers, by the publisher. Parties ordering by mail will please order by numbers.

**GEORGE MUNRO, Publisher,**

P. O. Box 3751.          17 to 27 Vandewater Street.

# WHAT IS SAPOLIO?

It is a solid, handsome cake of scouring soap, which has no equal for all cleaning purposes except the laundry. To use it is to value it.

What will Sapolio do? Why, it will clean paint, make oil-cloths bright, and give the floors, tables and shelves a new appearance.

It will take the grease off the dishes and off the pots and pans.

You can scour the knives and forks with it, and make the tin things shine brightly. The wash-basin, the bath-tub, even the greasy kitchen sink, will be as clean as a new pin if you use **SAPOLIO.** One cake will prove all we say. Be a clever little housekeeper and try it.

**BEWARE OF IMITATIONS.**

# THE SEASIDE LIBRARY.
## Pocket Edition.

The following books are for sale by all newsdealers, or will be sent to any address, postage prepaid, by the publisher, on receipt of 12 cents for single numbers, 17 cents for special numbers, and 25 cents for double numbers. Parties within reach of newsdealers will please get the books through them and thus avoid paying extra for postage. Those wishing the *Pocket Edition* of THE SEASIDE LIBRARY must be careful to mention the Pocket Edition, otherwise the Ordinary Edition will be sent. Address,

## GEORGE MUNRO, Publisher,
(P.O.Box 3751.)    17 to 27 Vandewater Street, N. Y.

| NO. | PRICE. |
|---|---|
| 1 Yolande. By William Black. .. | 20 |
| 2 Molly Bawn. By "The Duchess" ........ | 20 |
| 3 The Mill on the Floss. By George Eliot .... | 20 |
| 4 Under Two Flags. By "Ouida" | 20 |
| 5 The Admiral's Ward. By Mrs. Alexander. | 20 |
| 6 Portia. By "The Duchess" ... | 20 |
| 7 File No. 113. By Emile Gaboriau. | 20 |
| 8 East Lynne. By Mrs. Henry Wood.. | 20 |
| 9 Wanda, Countess von Szalras. By "Ouida" | 20 |
| 10 The Old Curiosity Shop. By Charles Dickens. | 20 |
| 11 John Halifax, Gentleman. By Miss Mulock. | 20 |
| 12 Other People's Money. By Emile Gaboriau. | 20 |
| 13 Eyre's Acquittal. By Helen B. Mathers | 10 |
| 14 Airy Fairy Lilian. By "The Duchess" | 10 |
| 15 Jane Eyre. By Charlotte Brontë | 20 |
| 16 Phyllis. By "The Duchess"... | 20 |
| 17 The Wooing O't. By Mrs. Alexander. | 15 |
| 18 Shandon Bells. By William Black. | 20 |
| 19 Her Mother's Sin. By the author of "Dora Thorne" | 10 |
| 20 Within an Inch of His Life. By Emile Gaboriau. | 20 |
| 21 Sunrise: A Story of These Times. By William Black. | 20 |
| 22 David Copperfield. By Charles Dickens. Vol. I | 20 |
| 22 David Copperfield. By Charles Dickens. Vol. II | 20 |
| 23 A Princess of Thule. By William Black. | 20 |
| 24 Pickwick Papers. By Charles Dickens. Vol. I | 20 |
| 24 Pickwick Papers. By Charles Dickens. Vol. II | 20 |
| 25 Mrs. Geoffrey. By "The Duchess" | 20 |
| 26 Monsieur Lecoq. By Emile Gaboriau. Vol. I | 20 |
| 26 Monsieur Lecoq. By Emile Gaboriau. Vol. II | 20 |
| 27 Vanity Fair. By William M. Thackeray. | 20 |
| 28 Ivanhoe. By Sir Walter Scott, Bart. | 20 |
| 29 Beauty's Daughters. By "The Duchess" | 10 |
| 30 Faith and Unfaith. By "The Duchess" | 20 |
| 31 Middlemarch. By George Eliot. | 20 |
| 32 The Land Leaguers. By Anthony Trollope. | 20 |
| 33 The Clique of Gold. By Emile Gaboriau. | 10 |
| 34 Daniel Deronda. By George Eliot. | 30 |
| 35 Lady Audley's Secret. By Miss M. E. Braddon. | 20 |
| 36 Adam Bede. By George Eliot .. | 20 |
| 37 Nicholas Nickleby. By Charles Dickens. | 30 |
| 38 The Widow Lerouge. By Emile Gaboriau .. | 20 |
| 39 In Silk Attire. By William Black. | 20 |
| 40 The Last Days of Pompeii. By Bulwer Lytton. | 20 |
| 41 Oliver Twist. By Charles Dickens. | 15 |
| 42 Romola. By George Eliot .... | 20 |

# THE SEASIDE LIBRARY.—Pocket Edition.

# THE SEASIDE LIBRARY.—Pocket Edition.

# THE SEASIDE LIBRARY.—Pocket Edition.

# THE SEASIDE LIBRARY.—Pocket Edition.

(7)

# THE SEASIDE LIBRARY.—Pocket Edition.

MUNRO'S PUBLICATIONS.

# THE SEASIDE LIBRARY

## ORDINARY EDITION.

### GEORGE MUNRO, PUBLISHER,
(P.O.Box 3751.)     17 to 27 Vandewater Street, N. Y

The following works contained in THE SEASIDE LIBRARY, Ordinary Edition are for sale by all newsdealers, or will be sent to any address, postage free, on receipt of 12 cents for single numbers, and 25 cents for double numbers, by the publisher. *Parties ordering by mail will please order by numbers.*

## MRS. ALEXANDER'S WORKS.

## WILLIAM BLACK'S WORKS.

## MISS M. E. BRADDON'S WORKS.

## CHARLOTTE, EMILY, AND ANNE BRONTE'S WORKS.

## LUCY RANDALL COMFORT'S WORKS.

## WILKIE COLLINS' WORKS.

## J. FENIMORE COOPER'S WORKS.

## CHARLES DICKENS' WORKS.

## ALEXANDER DUMAS' WORKS.

1842 The Iron Mask.  Second half............................ 20
1874 Piédouche, a French Detective...................... 20
1885 The Sculptor's Daughter.  First half.................... 20
1885 The Sculptor's Daughter.  Second half................. 20
1886 Zénobie Capitaine.  First half....................... 20
1886 Zénobie Capitaine.  Second half...................... 20
1925 Babiole, the Pretty Milliner.  First half................ 20

## EMILE GABORIAU'S WORKS.

 408 File No. 113............................................ 20
 465 Monsieur Lecoq.  First half........................... 20
 465 Monsieur Lecoq.  Second half......................... 20
 476 The Slaves of Paris.  First half........................ 20
 476 The Slaves of Paris.  Second half..................... 20
 490 Marriage at a Venture................................. 10
 494 The Mystery of Orcival................................ 20
 501 Other People's Money................................. 20
 509 Within an Inch of His Life ............................ 20
 515 The Widow Lerouge................................... 20
 523 The Clique of Gold.................................... 20
 671 The Count's Secret.  Part I....................... ..... 20
 671 The Count's Secret.  Part II........................... 20
 704 Captain Contanceau;  or, The Volunteers of 1792......... 10
 741 The Downward Path; or, A House Built on Sand (La De-
        gringolade).  Part I................................. 20
 741 The Downward Path; or, A House Built on Sand (La De-
        gringolade).  Part II ............................... 20
 758 The Little Old Man of the Batignolles.................. 10
 778 The Men of the Bureau................................ 10
 789 Promises of Marriage................................. 10
 813 The 13th Hussars..................................... 10
 834 A Thousand Francs Reward............................ 10
 899 Max's Marriage; or, The Vicomte's Choice .............. 10
1184 The Marquise de Brinvilliers........................... 20

## MARY CECIL HAY'S WORKS.

   8 The Arundel Motto.................................... 10
 407 The Arundel Motto (in large type)...................... 20
   9 Old Myddelton's Money............................... 10
 427 Old Myddelton's Money (in large type).................. 20
  17 Hidden Perils......................................... 10

## CHARLES LEVER'S WORKS.

## GEORGE MACDONALD'S WORKS.

www.ingramcontent.com/pod-product-compliance
Lightning Source LLC
Chambersburg PA
CBHW022337020726
47500CB00004B/1162